4 –

10/17
N

GOURMET
COFFEE, TEA
and
CHOCOLATE
DRINKS

GOURMET COFFEE, TEA
and
CHOCOLATE DRINKS

Creating Your Favorite
Recipes at Home

by Mathew Tekulsky

GRAMERCY BOOKS
NEW YORK

This 2002 edition published by Gramercy Books, an imprint of Random House Value Publishing, a division of Random House, Inc., 280 Park Avenue, New York, NY 10017, by arrangement with Crown Publishers, a division of Random House, Inc., and the author.

Gramercy is a registered trademark and the colophon is a trademark of Random House, Inc.

Printed in the United States

Random House
New York • Toronto • London • Sydney • Auckland
www.randomhouse.com

Library of Congress Cataloging-in-Publication Data

Tekulsky, Mathew, 1954-
    Gourmet coffee, tea and chocolate drinks : creating your favorite recipes at home /
by Mathew Tekulsky.
        p. cm.
    Reprint. Originally published in three volumes under titles: Coffee drinks. New York :
Crown, 1992. Tea drinks, 1995, and Chocolate drinks, 1996.
    ISBN 0-517-22118-7
    1. Coffee. 2. Tea. 3. Chocolate drinks. I. Title.

TX817.C6 T45 2002
641.8'77--dc21

                                                                              2002069286

9 8 7 6 5 4 3 2 1

Contents

MAKING YOUR OWN GOURMET COFFEE DRINKS

To Brandt Aymar

Acknowledgments

I would like to thank the following for their generous assistance in the writing of this book: Barnie's Coffee & Tea Company, Gloria Jean's Gourmet Coffees, Green Mountain Coffee Roasters, and Starbucks Coffee Company. Thanks as well to the Robert Bosch Corpora-  tion, Melitta, the Pasquini Espres- so Company, and Toddy Prod- ucts for their help. Thanks, as always, to my literary agent, Jane Jordan Browne, for her continued sup- port, and to my editor, Brandt Aymar, for his great advice. Finally, I wish to thank the friendly coffee servers at the many gourmet coffee shops that I visited during the course of writing this book. Their generous sharing of information on recipes and how certain drinks are made is greatly appreciated.

Contents

Introduction
9

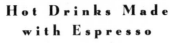

Introduction

For centuries, people have been enjoying coffee. From the Arabian and Turkish coffeehouses of the sixteenth century, on through the explosion of London's coffeehouses in the seventeenth century, citizens of the world have been brought together by their shared love of  this tasty and uplifting bever- age, as well as the charming companionship of like-minded friends. Even though coffeehouses ex- isted in Colo- nial America, it wasn't until af- ter the Boston Tea Party that coffee really became the national drink—which it has remained ever since. In the past few years, however, there has been a dramatic increase in the popularity of specialty coffee shops in the United States. Whereas people were once just inter- ested in having a standard cup of coffee, now they not only enjoy a regular espresso or cappuccino at the coffee bar, they're also *ordering specialty drinks with names such as Cappuccino Royale, Espresso con Panna, Mochaccino, and Latte Macchiato. And like wine connoisseurs, they are choosing coffee beans for home use with such names as Colombian Supremo, Ethiopian Harrar, Kona, and Jamaican Blue Mountain. Various specialty coffee shops also have their own house blends, or they may call a certain blend Gazebo, Andes Blend, or Swedish Supreme.*

With this book,  *you will not only learn how to brew a great cup of gourmet coffee at home,* **10** *using a variety of techniques, you will also discover how to incorporate this coffee into many of the most delicious gourmet coffee drinks that are being served in the best specialty coffee shops around the country today. And you will learn how to make many traditional coffee drinks that have been popular for generations. In addition, once you have tried the recipes included here, you will probably want to experiment on your own with different ingredients, depending on your own tastes. You may even come up with a few new gourmet coffee drinks!*

The Various Coffee Beans You Can Use

Before we start making drinks, we should learn a little bit about the various beans you can use, the type of equipment available for making coffee, and a few other useful tips that will help you do such things as keep your coffee fresh, grind the beans for maximum usability, steam your milk properly for cappuccinos, and prepare your iced coffee the right way.

Coffee comes from the seed of a coffee plant, which is processed and then roasted according to various specifications. The best coffee in the world comes from the *Coffea arabica* plant, which grows at high altitudes throughout the equatorial regions of the world.

Originally discovered growing wild in Ethiopia in ancient times, this plant was taken to Yemen by the Arabs and cultivated there as early as the sixth century. In the early 1700s, the Dutch began cultivating descendants of these original plants in Java, and from that time on, the cultivation of the *C. arabica* plant spread to many areas of Central America, South America, and Africa.

Another species of coffee plant, *Coffea robusta,* is also grown commercially (primarily in Africa), but this plant is used mostly for the lower grades of coffee that are on the market today.

Depending on where in the world your coffee is grown—from Indonesia to Central and South America, to Africa and the Middle East—it will have its own distinct taste and body. Coffee from Java, for instance, is earthy tasting and full-bodied, while beans from Costa Rica produce a lighter, more tangy cup of coffee. Columbian and Brazilian coffees are more middle-of-the-road types, providing a mild taste that can easily be blended with other beans. Coffee from Kenya, on the other hand, has a strong, winy taste.

Indeed, coffee from various regions of the same country will have its own unique flavor, depending on such factors as altitude, rainfall, and soil quality—and coffee from different plantations within the same region will even taste different from each other. Therefore, today's specialty coffee wholesalers and retailers send coffee tasters all over the world in search of the best-tasting coffee crop from each region.

After the green coffee beans are shipped to the United States, they must be roasted. This involves heating the beans at around 400°F. for about 5 to 15 minutes (depending on the temperature), while rotating them in large bins.

Most beans are light or medium roasted, producing a light- or medium-brown color and mild taste. Viennese or dark-roasted coffee produces a darker brown bean and an almost burnt (yet tangy) taste. The darkest roast (called espresso, Italian, or French) has a dark brown to almost black color and a burnt to charcoaly taste.

Coffee beans can also be blended to create desired effects. The combination of Mocha (a mild bean from Yemen) and Java, for instance, has become synonymous with the coffee drink itself. Other blends use a variety of different-tasting beans from various parts of the world, along with a variety of roasts. Hence, an excellent morning-coffee blend might include a majority of Viennese-roasted beans, along with half as much Mocha and a little bit of espresso roast just to spice things up. A good after-dinner blend, on the other hand, might include 50 percent Mocha-Java along with 25 percent each of Colombian and Costa Rican.

The proliferation of specialty coffee shops over the last few years has produced another new trend—that of flavored coffee beans. Thus, you'll find names such as Vanilla Nut, Chocolate Almond, and Irish Cream labeling bags of specially weighed and packaged coffees at your local shop (or you can order them by mail from the sources listed in the directory at the end of this book). Of course, you can always add flavorings or extracts to regular unflavored coffee after it's brewed, as the recipes that follow will indicate. Conversely, you may wish to use flavored coffees in any of the following recipes, being careful not to mix tastes that don't go together well.

In recent years, the quality of decaffeinated coffee has been rising significantly—at least on the gourmet level. Whereas in the past, lower-quality beans were commonly used for decaffeinated varieties, today there is no reason why you can't find a good-tasting decaffeinated coffee at a specialty coffee shop or elsewhere.

There are two basic types of decaffeination processes: one uses a solvent (most commonly methylene chloride) that clings to the caffeine and is then flushed away; another (the Swiss water process) uses repeated flushings of water to wash away the caffeine. The first process is generally acknowledged to produce a better-tasting cup of coffee (with virtually no chemical residue), while the Swiss water process is becoming increasingly popular because it uses no chemicals.

Storing Your Coffee Beans

Since coffee is a perishable food item, it is important to store your coffee beans properly before using them, if you want to make the best cup of coffee possible with the beans that you have.

In order to make the highest-quality cup of coffee, it is best to store your beans whole and grind them at home as you need them (see the section on grinding coffee, page 16).

Beans purchased in airtight (or vacuum-packed) bags will last for weeks or even months if unopened and stored at room temperature. Once the beans have been exposed to air, they should ideally be used within two weeks. Therefore, it is a good idea to buy your coffee on a regular basis, only as you need it.

When a bag of beans has been opened (or if the beans were purchased from an open bin at a specialty coffee shop), it should be stored in the freezer in an airtight container. They will remain fresh for a month or more. You can then take two weeks' worth of beans out of the freezer as you need them.

These beans should be stored in an airtight container at room temperature, or at about 60°F. (In warmer climates, they should be stored in the refrigerator.)

Ground coffee should be stored in an airtight container at room temperature (or in the refrigerator, depending on the climate), and for maximum freshness, it should be consumed within two weeks.

There are two basic types of coffee that we will be using in this book: brewed coffee and espresso.

Brewed coffee generally involves running hot water through coffee grounds, although it can be made using a cold-water process as well. Most brewed coffee is made with light- or medium-roast coffee, or with a dark roast like Viennese or French.

Espresso coffee describes not only the darkest roast of coffee bean (which is most often used for making espresso), but also the technique for making this type of coffee. Making espresso generally involves running hot water rapidly through finely ground espresso beans. This produces a small cup (or demitasse) of extremely strong-tasting coffee that usually needs to be sweetened with at least a little bit of sugar.

Tips for Making the Best Cup of Coffee

Here are a few tips for making the best cup of coffee possible with the equipment that you have:

1. Always use fresh water; your cup of coffee is only as good as the water that's used to make it.

2. In general, you should use 2 tablespoons of ground coffee for every 6 ounces of brewed coffee that you want to make. To make espresso, you generally use about 1 tablespoon of coffee for every $1\frac{1}{2}$ ounces of espresso.

3. Always use the proper grind for the equipment that you're using. Too fine a grind will cause overextraction, clogging of your filter, or small particles of coffee beans getting into your cup of coffee. Too coarse a grind will lead to underextraction and a weak, bitter cup of coffee as the water will go through the coffee too rapidly.

4. If you are using a manual device, use water that is just off the boil, so as not to "burn" the coffee.

5. Always serve your coffee immediately after you make it; never reheat your coffee or reuse your coffee grounds. (If you want to use your hot coffee later, pour it into a preheated thermos right after it's brewed.)

6. Be sure to clean your equipment regularly, so that coffee residues or mineral deposits don't build up that can ruin your future cups of coffee.

7. Never leave your coffee on the burner for more than 20 minutes. That will ruin it.

A Word About Filters

There are a number of different coffee filters available today, including those made with chlorine- or oxygen-bleached white paper, unbleached brown paper, or no paper at all (the so-called gold filter). The oxygen-bleached white filters are becoming increasingly popular because they are "friendly" to the environment. Brown filters, while also environmentally friendly, tend to leave a faint papery taste in the coffee. Gold filters (actually made of gold-plated steel) are desirable because they don't need to be replaced and don't filter out the natural oils of the coffee bean, as do the paper filters.

Grinding Coffee the Right Way

As explained earlier, it's extremely important to grind your coffee in the appropriate fashion, depending on the method of brewing that you're using.

The coarsest grind is used for percolators, French presses, and for the cold-water method of making coffee. Medium grinds are used for flat-bottomed drip makers and stove-top espresso makers. Fine grinds are used for cone-shaped drip filters, and very fine grinds are generally used for espresso machines. An extremely fine or powdery grind is used for making Turkish coffee in a jezve (see page 18).

Methods for Brewing Coffee

The method or methods you choose for making your coffee are largely a matter of personal preference, based on the taste of the coffee that each method produces, the ease of use of each technique, and even certain esthetic principles such as wanting to use a more traditional method rather than a modern one.

The most popular way of making coffee today is the *drip method*—either with a manual device by heating the water separately, or by using an electric machine. With the drip method, hot water is poured over the coffee grounds, which are placed in a filter above the carafe. This method offers convenience and a high-quality cup of coffee.

The *French press* (or plunger pot) method involves placing the coffee grounds at the bottom of a glass cylinder, pouring hot water over the grounds, letting them steep for 2 to 4 minutes, and then plunging a steel-mesh filter down to the bottom of the cylinder. This traps the grounds on the bottom and leaves the brewed coffee on top. Then you simply pour the coffee out of the carafe. The benefits of this method are that no paper filters are necessary and all of the coffee beans' essential oils remain in your cup of coffee—which is a rich one.

The *vacuum method* of making coffee consists of two glass pots that are placed one on top of the other and are connected by a glass tube with a filter. Water is placed in the bottom pot and coffee grounds in the top, and when the water is heated, it rises through the tube and spills over the grounds. When the pot is taken off of the heat source (be it a stove or a tabletop heat source), the brewed coffee falls back through the tube into the lower pot. This technique produces an extremely rich cup of coffee similar to that made with the French press method. However, it is much less commonly used.

Other methods for brewing coffee include using a *jezve,* the Neapolitan *flip-drip,* and the *percolator.*

The jezve is a long-handled brass or copper pot in which a small amount of water, coffee grounds, and usually sugar are placed, brought to a frothy boil, and then served in a demitasse cup. Often the froth is spooned into the cup twice before the coffee is poured out. This traditional (indeed, ancient) technique produces a rich, strong, almost muddy cup of coffee with plenty of grounds left on the bottom. You want to be careful to drink only the coffee, and not the grounds. (You can also make this type of coffee using a small saucepan.)

The Neapolitan flip-drip consists of two metal cylinders that are connected to each other, one on top of the other, with a filter in between. Water is placed in the bottom container and brought to a boil; then the entire device is turned upside down and the hot water drips down through ground coffee that has been placed in the filter. The now-bottom container has a spout through which the brewed coffee is poured. This technique produces a rich cup of coffee that tastes somewhat in between that produced by the gold filter and that produced by a stove-top espresso maker.

The percolator has become increasingly less popular in recent years, especially among gourmet coffee aficionados. This is because percolators not only boil the coffee but pass the heated water through the coffee grounds again and again. Because of this, the coffee's essential aroma and taste are basically burned out of it. The result is an often bitter cup of coffee.

One more method of brewing coffee should be discussed here: the *cold-water method.* With this process, cold water is added to very coarsely ground coffee in a large container and is allowed to steep for 10 to 24 hours, depending on how strong you want your coffee to be. Then the coffee is filtered into a carafe. It can be stored in the refrigerator for up to 3 weeks, this type of coffee can be drunk hot by using about $\frac{1}{3}$ cup of concentrate in every cup of hot water, or you can use it in iced coffee as you would extrastrength chilled coffee made with any hot-water process (see the following on making iced coffee). The result is a smooth, mild cup of coffee which is very low in acidity, as the cold-water process does not extract the oils of the coffee bean as thoroughly as does the hot-water process.

In order to make iced coffee using a standard hot-water brewing method, simply use $1\frac{1}{2}$ to 2 times the normal amount of coffee, brew it as you normally would, and pour it over ice—either immediately or after the coffee has cooled down to room temperature. It is best to use coffee made with this technique within 1 or 2 hours—no more than 3.

You can store this type of coffee in the refrigerator in a sealed container, but after about 1 day, the freshness and flavor of the coffee deteriorate dramatically. Therefore, it is always best to brew your iced coffee as soon as you can before drinking it. (You can also make coffee ice cubes with this mixture—or with cold-brewed coffee—that will not dilute your cup of iced coffee as will regular ice cubes.)

Making Espresso

There are basically two ways to make espresso: with a stove-top espresso maker or with an electric machine.

The stove-top espresso maker operates by heating water in the bottom chamber until it is forced up through the filter, which contains grounds of espresso roast coffee. Once the espresso reaches the top chamber, it can easily be poured out through the spout. A good steel stove-top espresso maker will make a quality demitasse of espresso in just a few minutes.

Some stove-top espresso makers also include a valve that can be used for steaming milk for cappuccinos. If you don't have one of these models, you can use an electric device that steams milk by heating water in a chamber and forcing it through a valve by steam pressure. (There is also a special stove-top device that you can use just for steaming milk.)

There are a number of electric espresso machines available today, and most of the less expensive ones are pretty comparable in terms of quality. The advantage here is that electric espresso machines also include a valve for steaming milk.

Cappuccino purists, however, may not be satisfied with the steaming capability of these less expensive machines, and may wish to purchase a more powerful espresso machine that approaches the commercial machines in terms of quality but is still affordable for the home user.

By contacting the manufacturers that are listed in the directory at the end of the book, you should be able to find just the right espresso machine for your purposes—and your budget.

Steaming Milk Properly

Perhaps a few words should be said here about how to steam milk properly with your home espresso machine for your cappuccinos and lattes.

In the first place, always start off with a cold pitcher (you can place it in the refrigerator beforehand). A stainless steel pitcher works best. Nonfat and low-fat milk are most widely used—although regular milk can be easily steamed once you get the hang of it.

Just fill the pitcher about one-third to one-half with the milk (no more than half, because the milk will expand when steamed). Place the nozzle of the steamer on the surface of the milk and turn the steam pressure all the way on.

As the steamer begins to froth the milk, lower the pitcher while the milk expands, keeping the nozzle about $\frac{1}{2}$ inch under the surface of the milk. Be careful not to let the milk boil, as it may overflow or have a bit of a burnt taste.

When the foam that you've produced by steaming the milk begins to rise to the surface of the pitcher, you can turn the pressure down or take the pitcher away from the steamer, as the milk is now just about to boil.

Ideally, steamed milk should contain very small bubbles throughout the liquid, and the foam on top should have a sweet or light taste to it. While steaming milk may seem rather awkward at first, with just a little bit of practice you'll really get the hang of it, and before long you should become an expert!

A Note on Ingredients

1. When not otherwise specified, regular granulated sugar (or other sweeteners, such as honey and brown sugar) can be added to any of these drinks, depending on your taste. Many of the drinks taste fine without any sugar at all. It's up to you.

2. It's always best to use fresh whipped cream—generally about $\frac{1}{4}$ cup per drink. Unless otherwise specified, whipped cream does not need to be sweetened, as you can sweeten the drink itself. However, if you wish to add a small amount of sugar to your whipped cream, there's no reason not to do so.

3. Low-fat or even nonfat milk can be substituted for whole milk, depending on your taste.

4. I use chocolate syrup in these recipes, but an equal amount of sweetened chocolate powder can be used as well. I also use sweetened chocolate powder as a topping, but if you're willing to make the effort, shaved or grated chocolate provides a more natural flavor. (Hint: Shave your chocolate slices beforehand and keep them in a sealed container in the refrigerator.)

5. I often use flavor extracts in these recipes, since these are the most readily available. Some specialty coffee shops carry flavored (and usually sweetened) syrups (or drops) that you can use in your gourmet coffee drinks. In general, 1 tablespoon of these flavored syrups (or a few drops) is the equivalent of $\frac{1}{4}$ teaspoon extract.

6. In the soda recipes, club soda can be substituted for carbonated (or sparkling) water.

7. If you wish to make more (or fewer) servings of these drinks, simply multiply (or divide) the amount of each ingredient to provide for the number of servings that you wish to make.

Once you understand the basics of good coffee making, it's time to start making drinks. This is simply a matter of mixing some of history's best flavors and spices with whatever type of coffee you like best at any given time of the day—or year, for that matter.

Perhaps you want a nice cappuccino in the morning, a delicious espresso after dinner, a tasty iced Caffè Latte (see page 42) on a hot summer afternoon, or a large mug of Viennese Coffee (see page 28) in front of the fireplace on a winter evening.

Throw in a little whipped cream, ice cream, carbonated water, or a slice of lemon or lime, depending on the drink you're making, and the combinations are virtually endless. You can even blend fresh fruit such as bananas, strawberries, and raspberries into your coffee drinks.

So why not get out your coffee maker and start making your own espressos, cappuccinos, lattes, mochas, and other gourmet coffee drinks in the comfort of your home. Just follow the recipes in these pages and you should be able to create a delicious gourmet coffee drink for just about any occasion.

Good luck! And, most of all, simply enjoy the results of your coffee-making efforts!

Hot

Drinks

Made

with

Brewed

Coffee

U*nless otherwise specified, all of the drinks in this chapter are made with freshly brewed coffee that is still hot, and should be served immediately.*

Café au Lait

This drink, popular throughout the world, enriches the standard cup of coffee with the delicate taste of steamed milk. You may wish to vary the proportions of coffee and milk, depending on your taste: for example, three-fourths coffee and one-fourth milk, or half coffee and half milk.

⅔ cup coffee
⅓ cup milk

Ground cinnamon or nutmeg, or sweetened chocolate powder (optional)

Pour the coffee into a cup. Steam the milk and add to the coffee, leaving a layer of foam on top. Sprinkle cinnamon, nutmeg, or chocolate powder on top of the foam, if desired.

Serves 1

Variation: For a Café Vermont, stir 3 tablespoons maple syrup into the coffee before adding the steamed milk. Proceed as directed above.

Café Mocha

This particular drink adds the taste of chocolate to a Café au Lait. As with the Café au Lait, the proportions of coffee and milk may be varied according to your taste.

⅔ cup coffee
*2 tablespoons chocolate
    syrup*

⅓ cup milk
*Sweetened chocolate
    powder (optional)*

Pour the coffee into a cup. Stir the chocolate syrup into the coffee. Steam the milk until hot and frothy, then add to the coffee, leaving a layer of foam on top. Sprinkle chocolate powder on top, if desired.

Serves 1

Variations: For a Café Mocha Mint, stir ⅛ teaspoon mint extract into the coffee along with the chocolate syrup. Proceed as directed above and garnish with a fresh mint sprig, if desired.

For a Mandarin Mocha, stir ⅛ teaspoon orange extract into the coffee along with the chocolate syrup. Proceed as directed above.

Viennese Coffee

A venerable tradition in Vienna's coffeehouses, this coffee's tasty flavor comes from the whipped cream topping.

2 cups coffee, preferably Viennese or other dark roast

*½ cup heavy cream, whipped
Ground cinnamon, nutmeg, or cloves*

Pour the coffee into 2 cups. Top each cup with a large dollop of whipped cream and sprinkle with cinnamon, nutmeg, or cloves.

Serves 2

Café Borgia

The citrus taste adds zest to this drink, while beautifully complementing the whipped cream at the same time.

*2 cups coffee
½ cup heavy cream, whipped*

Grated orange peel

Divide the coffee into 2 cups. Top each cup with a large dollop of whipped cream and sprinkle with grated orange peel.

Serves 2

Café Belgique

This drink has an enjoyable light vanilla taste, which is a result of the egg white mixture that rises to the surface of the cup.

1 egg white
½ cup heavy cream

¼ teaspoon vanilla extract
3 cups coffee

Beat the egg white until stiff. Whip the cream along with the vanilla. Mix the egg white and whipped cream mixture together and fill 4 cups one-third of the way. Add ⅔ cup coffee to each cup.

Serves 4

Chocolate Cream Coffee

Serve this drink in front of a fire on a cold winter evening.

¼ cup heavy cream
3 tablespoons chocolate
syrup
1 cup coffee

Ground cinnamon
Sweetened chocolate
powder
Grated orange peel

Whip all but 1 tablespoon of the cream. Stir the reserved tablespoon of cream and the chocolate syrup in a saucepan over low heat until mixed together. Add the coffee gradually, stirring the mixture as you do so. Pour into a mug and top with whipped cream and cinnamon, chocolate powder, and grated orange peel.

Serves 1

Spiced Cream Coffee

The spicy whipped cream is delicious, and combines with the chocolate-flavored coffee to create a great taste.

$\frac{3}{4}$ teaspoon ground
cinnamon
$\frac{1}{4}$ teaspoon ground
nutmeg
1 tablespoon sugar

$\frac{1}{2}$ cup heavy cream
$1\frac{1}{2}$ cups coffee
2 teaspoons chocolate
syrup

Stir $\frac{1}{4}$ teaspoon of the cinnamon and the nutmeg and sugar into the cream and whip. Divide the coffee into two 6-ounce portions and stir 1 teaspoon chocolate syrup and $\frac{1}{4}$ teaspoon cinnamon into each cup. Top with spiced whipped cream.

Serves 2

Spiced Coffee

Combining spices and coffee has been a tradition for as long as coffee has been consumed. You may want to experiment with your own combination—and amount—of spices.

$1\frac{1}{2}$ cups coffee
1 cinnamon stick
2 whole cloves
$\frac{1}{4}$ teaspoon whole allspice

$\frac{1}{2}$ cup heavy cream,
whipped
Ground cinnamon
White or brown sugar,
to taste

Pour the coffee over the cinnamon stick, cloves, and allspice in a saucepan and simmer over low heat for 5 to 7 minutes. Strain into cups, top with whipped cream, and sprinkle with cinnamon. Add white or brown sugar to taste.

Serves 2

Variation : Omit the cinnamon stick and allspice and substitute 2 strips each of orange and lemon peel; use 10 cloves instead of 2. Proceed as directed above.

Café Vanilla

This drink is fun to make, and the natural flavor of the vanilla bean is a nice reward that you can taste with each sip. If you use an espresso or other dark roast when you brew your coffee, you can approximate the taste of a cappuccino with this drink.

¼ *vanilla bean*	¾ *cup coffee*
½ *cup milk*	*Ground cinnamon or*
1 teaspoon brown sugar	*nutmeg*

Slice the vanilla bean lengthwise and place it with the milk and brown sugar in a saucepan. Bring to a boil, stirring occasionally. Remove from the heat, cover, and let stand for a few minutes. Take out the vanilla bean and blend the milk mixture in a blender for about 30 seconds, or until it becomes frothy. Add to the hot coffee and top with cinnamon or nutmeg.

Serves 1

Cinnamon-Vanilla Coffee

Here the taste of cinnamon is added to that of vanilla to make for a delightful taste combination. The brown sugar–whipped cream topping gives it a little extra pizzazz!

1½ cups coffee
¼ vanilla bean, sliced
1 cinnamon stick

½ cup heavy cream
1 tablespoon or more
brown sugar

Before brewing the coffee, slice the vanilla bean lengthwise and place it with the cinnamon stick in the bottom of the coffee maker carafe. While the coffee is brewing, whip the cream and brown sugar together. Pour the coffee into 2 cups and top with the whipped cream mixture. Add extra brown sugar to taste, if desired.

Serves 2

Chocolate-Vanilla Coffee

Chocolate and vanilla are a natural taste combination—each complements the other. You can pour over ice for a cool taste, too!

1 tablespoon chocolate
syrup
¼ teaspoon vanilla extract

1 cup coffee
¼ cup heavy cream,
whipped

Stir the chocolate syrup and vanilla into the hot coffee. Top with whipped cream.

Serves 1

Coffee Grog

The addition of brown sugar and butter makes this spicy drink even richer, while orange and lemon peel give it just the extra flavor it needs.

2 tablespoons butter

1 cup brown sugar

⅛ teaspoon ground allspice

⅛ teaspoon ground cinnamon

⅛ teaspoon ground nutmeg

⅛ teaspoon ground cloves

1½ cups heavy cream or half-and-half

12 small strips of orange peel

12 small strips of lemon peel

9 cups coffee

1½ teaspoons rum extract (optional)

Melt the butter in a saucepan over low heat. Stir in the brown sugar, allspice, cinnamon, nutmeg, and cloves, and allow the mixture to cool. Store in a sealed container in the refrigerator.

To serve, combine in each cup 1 teaspoon of the butter mixture, 2 tablespoons cream, 1 strip orange peel, and 1 strip lemon peel. Add 6 ounces of hot coffee and stir. You can also add ⅛ teaspoon rum extract to each cup of grog, if desired.

Serves 12

Variation: Omit the allspice and cinnamon and double the amount of ground nutmeg and cloves. Proceed as directed above.

Turkish Coffee

The fun of making Turkish coffee lies in the use of the jezve (see page 18). Conjuring up images of the ancient Middle East as you make your coffee will prepare you for the strong taste of the coffee as you sip it. (Be careful not to drink the grounds!) This method of making coffee is common throughout the Middle East, and should more accurately be called Middle Eastern coffee. Some of the best beans to use are Mocha, Java, and Viennese roast.

1 tablespoon extremely fine ground or powdered coffee

½ to 2 teaspoons sugar (optional)

2 ounces cold water

In a jezve, stir all the ingredients together. Place over low heat and slowly bring this mixture to a boil (do not stir). When it reaches the boiling point, remove from the heat and pour into a demitasse. Let the grounds settle before drinking, or add a tiny splash of cold water to help settle the grounds.

Serves 1

Variations: For a frothier drink, let the coffee foam up, remove the pot from the heat, and spoon the top froth into your cup. Return the pot to the fire and repeat twice more, then pour the liquid into the cup. For interesting taste sensations, add ⅛ teaspoon ground cardamom, cinnamon, nutmeg, or cloves to the ground coffee before brewing. For a rich, creamy drink, use milk instead of water.

Hawaiian Coffee

Try this tropical drink on a warm summer evening, or use it to warm yourself up on a cold winter day.

$\frac{1}{2}$ cup milk $\frac{1}{2}$ cup coffee
$\frac{1}{2}$ cup sweetened shredded
  coconut

Preheat the oven to 350°F. Place the milk and coconut in a saucepan and warm over low heat for 2 to 3 minutes, stirring occasionally. Strain the milk and place the coconut on a baking sheet in the oven until it turns brown, about 8 to 10 minutes. Add the milk to the hot coffee and top with the browned coconut.

Serves 1

New Orleans Coffee

The secret of this coffee is the earthy taste of the chicory. Use a dark roast of coffee, and mix the chicory into the ground coffee before brewing as usual. You may want to vary the proportions of coffee and milk, for example using two-thirds coffee and one-third milk, or one-third coffee and two-thirds milk. The amount of chicory can also vary, from 20 to 40 percent, depending on your taste.

1 cup coffee, with 25
percent ground chicory

1 cup steamed milk
Ground cinnamon

Pour the coffee into two cups. Add steamed milk evenly to both and top off each cup with some froth from the steamed milk. Sprinkle cinnamon on top.

Serves 2

Spiced Coffee Cider

On a crisp autumn afternoon, have some fun making this coffee, and then sit back and enjoy its taste.

$\frac{1}{2}$ cup coffee
$\frac{1}{2}$ cup apple juice
1 cinnamon stick
1 thin slice of orange,
including rind

$\frac{1}{8}$ teaspoon ground cloves
$\frac{1}{8}$ teaspoon ground allspice
1 teaspoon brown sugar
Ground cinnamon
(optional)

Stir all the ingredients except cinnamon together in a saucepan and simmer over low heat for 3 to 4 minutes, stirring occasionally. Strain into a mug and sprinkle with cinnamon, if desired.

Serves 1

Blended Banana Coffee

Drink this concoction as soon as you can after making it—before it has time to settle.

1 tablespoon butter
½ banana, peeled, sliced, and mashed
½ teaspoon ground cinnamon

¼ teaspoon vanilla extract
1 cup hot coffee
½ cup heavy cream
1 tablespoon confectioners' sugar

Melt the butter in a saucepan over low heat. Stir in the banana, cinnamon, and vanilla. Simmer for 1 to 2 minutes, stirring occasionally. Remove from the heat. Place the coffee, cream, and sugar in the blender and add the banana mixture. Blend for 15 to 20 seconds, or until smooth. Serve at once.

Serves 1

H o t

Drinks

M a d e

with

E s p r e s s o

A*ll of the drinks in this section begin with a basic espresso drink. From this starting point, the combinations are virtually endless.* *The following drinks represent the most popular among those that are served in today's gourmet coffee shops— and include many traditional favorites as well.* *Experiment all you want with the amount and strength of the espresso that you use in each drink, as well as with any of the other ingredients —milk, flavors, and spices.* *The rewards will be there for you with every sip.* *Enjoy!*

E s p r e s s o : An espresso consists of about 1½ ounces of extremely strong-tasting coffee. It is made with a dark-roasted bean, using either a stove-top espresso maker or an electric machine. It serves as the basis for many gourmet coffee drinks, both hot and cold, and has numerous variations of its own. Add almond, rum, brandy, mint, or vanilla extract to taste, if desired. You can also sprinkle spices such as ground cinnamon and cardamom onto your espresso.

D o u b l e   E s p r e s s o : Use twice the amount of water and coffee grounds as you would for a single espresso.

R i s t r e t t o : Use the same amount of grounds as for a single espresso, but stop the flow of water at about 1 ounce. This is also known as a "short" espresso.

Espresso Romano: A single espresso served with a small slice of lemon peel.

Espresso Anise: A single espresso with $\frac{1}{8}$ teaspoon anise extract added. For an Espresso Anise Royale, top with whipped cream.

Americano: A single espresso with hot water added to taste (usually about 1 cup).

Red Eye: A single espresso added to 1 cup brewed coffee.

Macchiato: A single espresso with a dollop of foam from steamed milk (1 to 2 tablespoons) on top.

Espresso con Panna: A single espresso topped with whipped cream.

Espresso Borgia: A single espresso topped with whipped cream (or froth from steamed milk) and grated orange peel.

Espresso Grog: Prepare a grog mixture as described in the recipe for Coffee Grog (see page 33). For each cup of Espresso Grog, place 1 teaspoon of the grog mixture in the bottom of the cup, along with 1 tablespoon heavy cream (or half-and-half), 1 small strip orange peel, and 1 small strip lemon peel. Add a single espresso to each of these cups and stir in the grog mixture thoroughly. You can also add a tiny amount (less than $\frac{1}{8}$ teaspoon) of rum extract to each cup of grog, if desired.

Makes 12 servings

C a p p u c c i n o : This drink consists of one-third espresso (a single) and one-third steamed milk, and is topped with one-third foam from the steamed milk. Sprinkle ground cinnamon, nutmeg, or sweetened chocolate powder on top, if desired. You can also add almond, rum, brandy, mint, or vanilla extract to taste. For a Double Cappuccino, use a double espresso instead of a single.

C a p p u c c i n o   R o y a l e : A cappuccino topped with whipped cream, and often with almond, rum, brandy, mint, or vanilla extract added to taste. Garnish with a thin wafer.

B u t t e r s c o t c h   C a p p u c c i n o : Add butterscotch syrup to a cappuccino to taste. For a Butterscotch Latte, do the same thing with a Caffè Latte.

C a f f è   L a t t e : This drink consists of a single espresso with the rest of the glass filled up with steamed milk, and is topped off with a thin layer of foam from the steamed milk. Sprinkle ground cinnamon, nutmeg, or sweetened chocolate powder on top, if desired. You can also add almond, rum, brandy, mint, or vanilla extract to taste. For a Double Caffè Latte, use a double espresso instead of a single.

L a t t e   M a c c h i a t o : Put steamed milk, topped with foam from the steamed milk into a glass; then gently pour a single espresso into the glass. The espresso will slowly drip to the bottom.

M o c h a c c i n o : This drink consists of one-third espresso (a single), one-third steamed chocolate milk, and one-third foam from the steamed chocolate milk for topping. (You can also make this drink by stirring chocolate syrup into the espresso, adding one-third steamed milk, and topping it off with one-third foam from the steamed milk.) Top with whipped cream and sweetened chocolate powder, if desired. For a Double Mochaccino, use a double espresso instead of a single.

Mocha Latte: This drink consists of a single espresso with the rest of the glass filled up with steamed chocolate milk, and topped off with a thin layer of foam from the steamed chocolate milk. (You can also make this drink by stirring chocolate syrup into the espresso, filling up the rest of the glass with steamed milk, and topping it off with a thin layer of foam from the steamed milk.) Top with whipped cream and sweetened chocolate powder, if desired. For a Double Mocha Latte, use a double espresso instead of a single.

Spiced Chocolate Espresso

The taste of espresso comes alive in this spicy drink.

2 double espressos
(page 40)
2 ounces heavy cream or
half-and-half
$\frac{1}{4}$ teaspoon ground
cinnamon

$\frac{1}{8}$ teaspoon ground nutmeg
2 teaspoons sugar
2 teaspoons chocolate syrup
Whipped cream

Mix all the ingredients except the chocolate syrup and whipped cream in a pitcher and steam until hot and frothy. Pour into 2 mugs, add 1 teaspoon chocolate syrup to each, and stir. Top with whipped cream.

Serves 2

Cold

Drinks

Made

with

Brewed

Coffee

Unless otherwise specified, all of the drinks in this section are made with cold coffee. In order to account for the dilution factor of ice cubes, you should brew coffee using one-and-a-half times to twice the amount of ground coffee per cup than normal. Then store the coffee in a sealed container in the refrigerator.

Iced Mint Coffee

Enjoy the minty taste of this cool drink on a warm summer evening.

$\frac{1}{2}$ cup coffee
$\frac{1}{8}$ teaspoon mint extract
1 tablespoon heavy cream, or $\frac{1}{4}$ cup milk or half-and-half

Ice cubes
Fresh mint sprig, for garnish

Mix together the coffee, mint, and cream. Pour over ice. Garnish with a fresh mint sprig.

Serves 1

Variations: Omit the cream and proceed as directed above, or omit the mint extract and mint sprig and substitute $\frac{1}{8}$ teaspoon almond, rum, brandy, or vanilla extract.

Iced Café au Lait

The foam on top of this drink provides a delicate taste through which to drink your coffee.

Ice cubes
⅔ cup coffee

⅓ cup milk

Fill a glass with ice. Pour in the coffee. Steam the milk and pour into the glass, leaving a layer of foam on top.

Serves 1

Iced Almond Coffee

Here's a sweet drink with a little treat to top it off!

4 cups coffee
2 cups half-and-half
4 tablespoons sweetened
  condensed milk
2 tablespoons sugar

1 teaspoon almond extract
Ice cubes
1 cup heavy cream, whipped
  Sliced almonds, for
garnish

Mix the coffee, half-and-half, condensed milk, sugar, and almond in a pitcher. Pour over ice in 4 glasses or mugs. Top each portion with whipped cream and garnish with a few slices of almond.

Serves 4

Spiced Iced Coffee I

The combination of spices and coffee works just as well in cold drinks as in hot ones. This and the following recipes should give you some ideas for spice mixtures. You may also want to experiment on your own, depending on which spices you like best.

1½ cups freshly brewed coffee

1½ tablespoons sugar

1 cinnamon stick

3 whole cloves

⅛ teaspoon ground allspice

Ice cubes

Whipped cream (optional)

Place all the ingredients except the ice and whipped cream in a saucepan and warm over low heat. Stir until the sugar is dissolved. Let the mixture cool to room temperature, about 30 minutes. Remove the cinnamon stick and cloves, and pour over ice. Top with whipped cream, if desired.

Serves 2

Spiced Iced Coffee II

Here is another, slightly different method of making spiced coffee ahead of time, to serve whenever you wish.

2 cinnamon sticks	4 cups freshly brewed coffee
4 whole cloves	Ice cubes
¼ teaspoon whole allspice	Milk (optional)
¼ teaspoon cardamom seeds	Brown sugar (optional)

Place the cinnamon sticks, cloves, allspice, and cardamom seeds at the bottom of a container, and pour coffee over the spices. Let the mixture cool to room temperature, about 30 minutes. Strain into a new container and store in the refrigerator.

When ready to serve, pour over ice and add milk and brown sugar, if desired.

Serves 4 to 6

Variation: Omit the four spices and add 4 strips each of orange and lemon peel, and 8 cloves. Proceed as directed above.

Iced Cardamom Coffee

Cardamom works just as well with cold coffee as with hot. You can pretend you're in a Middle Eastern bazaar while you drink this one.

½ teaspoon cardamom seeds

2 cups water

4 tablespoons coffee grounds

Ice cubes

Sugar, to taste

Lemon or pineapple slices, or maraschino cherries, for garnish

Boil the cardamom seeds in the water for about 5 minutes. Strain and use this water to brew your coffee. Pour the coffee over ice and sweeten with sugar to taste. Garnish with slices of lemon or pineapple or with maraschino cherries.

Serves 2

Honey Iced Coffee

This is a smooth, sweet drink. If you stir the honey in first, you'll avoid having it harden after the ice is added.

Honey, to taste

1 cup freshly brewed coffee

Ice cubes

Whipped cream (optional)

Ground cinnamon and nutmeg

Stir the honey into the coffee to taste. Add ice and top with whipped cream, if desired. Sprinkle with cinnamon and nutmeg.

Serves 1

Iced Maple Coffee

On a hot day, try this drink for a great taste of Vermont.

3 tablespoons maple syrup
*1 cup freshly brewed
  coffee*

Ice cubes
*¼ cup heavy cream,
  whipped*

Stir the maple syrup into the coffee and pour over ice. Top with whipped cream.

Serves 1

Iced Coffee Bitters

Bitters add a tangy taste to this cooling drink.

½ teaspoon bitters
1 teaspoon vanilla extract
4 tablespoons sugar
4½ cups coffee

Ice cubes
*Whipped cream or half-
and-half (optional)*

Mix the bitters, vanilla, and sugar together with 2 tablespoons of the coffee until the mixture is a thick syrup. Add 2½ teaspoons of this mixture to every 6 ounces of coffee. Serve over ice. Top with whipped cream or lightly pour 2 tablespoons half-and-half onto the top of each drink, if desired.

Serves 6

Coffee Soda

Adding carbonated water to coffee provides a nice sparkle for your drinks. The fruit garnish supplies a little punch as well.

½ cup coffee
Ice cubes
¼ cup carbonated water (or cola)

Strip of lemon, orange, or lime peel, for garnish

Pour the coffee over ice. Add carbonated water and garnish with a small strip of lemon, orange, or lime peel.

Serves 1

Coffee Ice Cream Soda

The addition of ice cream creates a frosty, old-fashioned treat.

½ cup coffee
1 ounce half-and-half (optional)
Ice cubes

¼ cup carbonated water (or cola)
1 scoop vanilla ice cream

Pour the coffee and half-and-half, if desired, over ice in a tall glass. Add the carbonated water and ice cream.

Serves 1

Variations: Substitute 1 scoop of chocolate or coffee ice cream for the vanilla. Proceed as directed above.

Rum Coffee Soda

With the taste of rum, you can pretend you're in the Caribbean.

1 cup coffee
¼ cup half-and-half
¼ teaspoon rum extract

Ice cubes
½ cup carbonated water
Sugar, to taste

Mix the coffee, half-and-half, and rum together and pour over ice in two tall glasses. Add carbonated water and sugar to taste.

Serves 2

Chocolate Coffee Float

This is another time-honored drink that actually tastes as good as it sounds.

2 scoops chocolate
ice cream
1 cup coffee

¼ cup heavy cream, whipped
Sweetened chocolate
powder

Add the ice cream to the coffee in a tall glass. Top with whipped cream and chocolate powder.

Serves 1

Variations: Substitute 2 scoops of vanilla or coffee ice cream for the chocolate. Proceed as directed above.

Hot Coffee Float

Hot coffee is the secret to the success of this drink. As the ice cream melts, all of the tastes blend together.

1 scoop each vanilla, chocolate, and coffee ice cream

¾ cup freshly brewed coffee, still piping hot

¼ cup heavy cream, whipped

Place the scoops of ice cream in a tall glass and add the coffee. Top with the whipped cream.

Serves 1

Blended Vanilla Coffee

A light, fluffy drink, this has a smooth vanilla taste.

½ cup coffee

1 cup milk

½ teaspoon vanilla extract

1 tablespoon sugar

Ice cubes

Ground cinnamon (optional)

Mix all the ingredients except the ice and cinnamon in a blender for 15 to 20 seconds, or until frothy. Pour over ice in a tall glass, and top with a dash of cinnamon, if desired.

Serves 1

Blended Chocolate Coffee

Here's another light, fluffy drink, this time with a smooth, chocolaty taste.

½ cup coffee

2 cups milk

2 tablespoons chocolate
  syrup

1 tablespoon sugar

Ice cubes

Whipped cream (optional)

Sweetened chocolate
  powder (optional)

Mix the coffee, milk, chocolate syrup, and sugar in a blender for 15 to 20 seconds, or until frothy. Pour over ice in 2 tall glasses and top with whipped cream and chocolate powder, if desired.

Serves 2

Blended Honey Coffee

For an easy but good cup of coffee first thing in the morning, try this one.

¾ cup coffee

¾ cup milk

1 tablespoon honey

Mix all the ingredients together in a blender for 10 to 15 seconds.

Serves 1

Banana Coffee Blend

Serve this drink right away, before it has time to settle.

1 cup coffee

1 cup milk

1 banana, peeled and sliced

1 tablespoon confectioners'
sugar

Mix all the ingredients together in a blender for 15 to 20 seconds, or until smooth.

Serves 1

Coffee Crush

This is best consumed immediately.

$\frac{3}{4}$ cup coffee

$1\frac{1}{4}$ cups crushed ice

Sugar to taste

Ice cubes

Whipped cream
(optional)

Sweetened chocolate
powder, ground
cinnamon or nutmeg
(optional)

Mix the coffee, crushed ice, and sugar in a blender for 15 to 20 seconds, or until frothy. Pour over ice, top with whipped cream, and sprinkle with chocolate powder, cinnamon, or nutmeg, if desired.

Serves 2

Chocolate-Coffee Crush

A favorite in most of today's gourmet coffee shops, this tastes like a chocolate-coffee milkshake.

$\frac{3}{4}$ cup coffee	Sugar, to taste
$\frac{1}{2}$ cup milk	Whipped cream (optional)
$\frac{1}{2}$ cup crushed ice	Sweetened chocolate
2 tablespoons	powder (optional)
chocolate syrup	

Mix all the ingredients except the whipped cream and chocolate powder in a blender for 15 to 20 seconds, or until smooth. Pour into a tall glass and top with whipped cream and chocolate powder, if desired.

Serves 1

Variations: For a Vanilla-Coffee Crush, omit the chocolate syrup and substitute $\frac{1}{4}$ teaspoon vanilla extract. Proceed as directed above.

For a Creamy Coffee Crush, simply omit the chocolate syrup.

Vanilla-Chocolate Coffee Shake

The hint of cinnamon makes this a delicious drink.

½ cup coffee
*1 tablespoon chocolate
 syrup*
2 scoops vanilla ice cream

*⅛ teaspoon ground
 cinnamon*
*Whipped cream
 (optional)*

Mix all the ingredients except the whipped cream in a blender for 15 to 20 seconds, or until smooth. Top with whipped cream, if desired.

Serves 1

58

Variations: For a Chocolate Coffee Shake, omit the vanilla ice cream and cinnamon and substitute 2 scoops of chocolate ice cream and ⅛ teaspoon ground nutmeg. Proceed as directed above.

For a Coffee Coffee Shake, substitute 2 scoops of coffee ice cream for the vanilla ice cream and cinnamon.

Vanilla-Banana Coffee Shake

You will savor every sip of this creamy, rich shake.

½ cup coffee
⅓ banana, peeled and sliced
2 scoops vanilla ice cream
⅛ teaspoon almond extract

*⅛ teaspoon ground
 cinnamon*
*Whipped cream
 (optional)*

Mix all the ingredients except the whipped cream in a blender for 15 to 20 seconds, or until smooth. Top with whipped cream, if desired.

Serves 1

Vanilla-Rum Coffee Shake

The rum gives this drink a delightful flavor.

1½ cups coffee

½ teaspoon rum extract

2 scoops vanilla ice cream

Ice cubes

Mix all the ingredients except the ice in a blender for 15 to 20 seconds, or until smooth. Pour over ice in tall glasses.

Serves 2

Yogurt Coffee Shake

This drink is a perfect treat at lunch.

½ cup coffee

1 cup vanilla yogurt

¼ teaspoon vanilla extract

1 teaspoon confectioners' sugar

Mix all the ingredients together in a blender for 15 to 20 seconds, or until smooth.

Serves 1

Butterscotch Coffee Shake

For butterscotch lovers, this drink is a natural.

5 ounces coffee

$2\frac{1}{4}$ tablespoons heavy cream

1 scoop vanilla (or coffee)
ice cream

2 tablespoons butterscotch
syrup

Mix all the ingredients together in a blender for 15 to 20 seconds, or until smooth.

Serves 1

Tropical Coffee Delight

You will enjoy sipping this drink slowly on a hot summer day.

$\frac{1}{2}$ cup coffee

$\frac{1}{4}$ cup papaya nectar

$\frac{1}{2}$ kiwi fruit, peeled and
sliced

1 tablespoon cream of
coconut

1 scoop vanilla ice cream

3–4 tablespoons heavy cream
(optional)

Mix the coffee, papaya, $\frac{1}{4}$ kiwi, coconut, and ice cream in a blender for 15 to 20 seconds, or until smooth. Garnish with the remaining kiwi and pour the heavy cream lightly on top, if desired.

Serves 1

Strawberry Delight

The combination of coffee, cream, and strawberries (or other fresh fruit) makes this a very unique drink, in all of its variations.

½ cup heavy cream

½ cup coffee

4 strawberries

¼ teaspoon almond extract

Confectioners' sugar, to taste

Additional strawberries, for garnish

Ice cubes (optional)

Whip ¼ cup of the cream and set aside. Mix the coffee, remaining cream, 4 strawberries, almond, and sugar in a blender for 15 to 20 seconds, or until smooth. Top with the whipped cream and garnish with fresh strawberries. (You can also pour this drink over ice, if desired.)

Serves 1

Variations: For a Raspberry Delight, omit the strawberries and substitute 12 raspberries. Proceed as directed above. Garnish with fresh raspberries.

For a Kiwi Delight, substitute 1 kiwi fruit, peeled and sliced, for the strawberries. Proceed as directed above. Garnish with a few slices of kiwi.

Cold
Drinks
Made
with
Espresso

All of the drinks in this section begin with a basic espresso drink. In most cases, you'll be able to use freshly made espresso, since the amount you'll be using for each drink will be small enough to allow it to cool quickly when poured over ice. If you let the espresso cool down for a few minutes after making it, less ice will melt and you'll end up with a cooler drink. You may want to make a large batch of espresso and store it in a sealed container in the refrigerator. However, as with brewed coffee, after about a day the freshness and flavor of the espresso will deteriorate dramatically. Therefore, when using espresso in cold drinks, it is best to make the espresso as late as you can before drinking it. Since cold drinks are usually consumed in larger quantities than are hot drinks, you may wish to use double espressos for many of these drinks. However, as with hot espresso drinks, you should experiment with the volume and strength of the espresso that you use, as well as with any of the other ingredients, such as milk, flavors, and spices. Here are some favorites as well as traditional coffees that are available in most gourmet coffee shops around the country. Salut!

Iced Espresso: A single or double espresso poured over ice cubes. Garnish with a small slice of lemon peel, if desired.

Iced Americano: Add hot water to a single espresso to taste, then pour over ice cubes.

Iced Macchiato: An iced espresso with a dollop of foam from steamed milk (1 to 2 tablespoons) on top.

Iced Espresso con Panna: An iced espresso topped with whipped cream.

Iced Maple Espresso: Stir 2 tablespoons maple syrup into a single espresso. Pour over ice cubes and top with whipped cream, if desired. For a Double Iced Maple Espresso, use twice the amount of maple syrup and espresso as for a single.

Iced Cappuccino: This drink consists of one-third espresso (a single), one-third cold milk, and one-third foam topping from steamed milk, over ice cubes. Sprinkle ground cinnamon or nutmeg or sweetened chocolate powder on top, and garnish with a fresh mint leaf, if desired. You can also add almond, rum, brandy, mint, or vanilla extract to taste. For a Double Iced Cappuccino, use a double espresso instead of a single.

Iced Cappuccino Royale: An iced cappuccino topped with whipped cream and garnished with a thin wafer. Add almond, rum, brandy, mint, or vanilla extract to taste, if desired.

Iced Caffè Latte: Pour a single espresso over ice cubes in a tall glass. Fill the rest of glass with cold milk and top with a thin layer of foam from steamed milk. Sprinkle ground cinnamon or nutmeg or sweetened chocolate powder on top, and garnish with a mint leaf, if desired. You can also add almond, rum, brandy, mint, or vanilla extract to taste. For a Double Iced Caffè Latte, use a double espresso instead of a single.

Iced Mochaccino: This drink consists of one-third espresso (a single), one-third cold chocolate milk, and one-third foam topping from steamed chocolate (or regular) milk, over ice cubes. Top with whipped cream and sweetened chocolate powder, if desired. For a Double Iced Mochaccino, use a double espresso instead of a single.

Iced Mocha Latte: Pour a single espresso over ice cubes in a tall glass. Fill the rest of glass with cold chocolate milk. Add a thin layer of foam from steamed chocolate (or regular) milk and top with whipped cream and sweetened chocolate powder, if desired. For a Double Iced Mocha Latte, use a double espresso instead of a single.

Espresso Soda

This drink is refreshing and surprisingly strong.

Single espresso (page 40)
Ice cubes
½ cup carbonated water (or cola)

Lemon, orange, or lime peel, for garnish

Pour the espresso over ice. Add carbonated water and garnish with a small piece of lemon, orange, or lime peel.

Serves 1

Variation: For a Double Espresso Soda, use double the amount of espresso and carbonated water (or cola).

Rum Espresso Soda

The rum flavor gives this drink an exotic taste.

Single espresso (page 40)
¼ cup heavy cream
¼ teaspoon rum extract

Ice cubes
½ cup carbonated water
Sugar, to taste

Mix the espresso, cream, and rum together and pour over ice. Add the carbonated water and sugar to taste.

Serves 1

Blended Honey Latte

This drink, you will find, is a great pick-me-up.

> *Single espresso (page 40)* *1 teaspoon honey*
> *¾ cup milk*

Mix all the ingredients together in a blender for 10 to 15 seconds.

Serves 1

Espresso Float

This is a perfect dessert—sweet, and filling.

> *Double espresso (page 40)* *Sweetened chocolate powder*
> *¼ cup milk*
> *2 scoops vanilla ice cream* *1 cinnamon stick, for garnish*
> *¼ cup heavy cream, whipped*

Pour the espresso into a tall glass. Add the milk and ice cream and top with whipped cream and chocolate powder. Garnish with the cinnamon stick.

Serves 1

Variations: Instead of vanilla ice cream, use 2 scoops of chocolate or coffee ice cream. Proceed as directed above.

For a Cappuccino Float, use a hot or iced cappuccino with 1 scoop of vanilla ice cream. For a Chocoloccino, use chocolate ice cream.

For a Mochaccino Float, use a hot or iced mochaccino with 1 scoop of vanilla ice cream.

Espresso Ice Cream Soda

This drink is sure to satisfy.

Single espresso (page 40)
1 ounce half-and-half
   (optional)
Ice cubes

$\frac{1}{2}$ cup carbonated water (or
   cola)
1 scoop vanilla ice cream

Pour espresso and half-and-half, if desired, over ice. Add carbonated water and ice cream.

Serves 1

Espresso Crush

Whipped cream makes this drink much richer.

Double espresso
(page 40)
$\frac{1}{2}$ cup crushed ice
Sugar, to taste
Ice cubes

Whipped cream (optional)
Sweetened chocolate
powder, ground
cinnamon or nutmeg
(optional)

Mix the espresso, crushed ice, and sugar in a blender for 15 to 20 seconds, or until frothy. Pour over ice. If desired, top with whipped cream and sprinkle with chocolate powder, cinnamon, or nutmeg.

Serves 1

Chocolate Espresso Crush

You may wish to use two scoops of ice cream instead of crushed ice in this drink, which is like an espresso shake.

*Double espresso
(page 40)
¼ cup milk
½ cup crushed ice
2 tablespoons chocolate
syrup*

*Sugar, to taste
Whipped cream (optional)
Sweetened chocolate
powder (optional)*

Mix all the ingredients except the whipped cream and chocolate powder in a blender for 15 to 20 seconds, or until smooth. Top with whipped cream and chocolate powder, if desired.

Serves 1

Variations: For a Vanilla Espresso Crush, substitute ⅛ teaspoon vanilla extract for the chocolate syrup.

For a Creamy Espresso Crush, omit the chocolate syrup.

Tropical Espresso Delight

This sweet, tangy drink still has the taste of espresso coming through.

Single espresso
(page 40)

$\frac{1}{8}$ cup papaya nectar

1 teaspoon cream of
coconut

$\frac{1}{4}$ kiwi fruit, peeled and
sliced

$\frac{1}{2}$ scoop vanilla ice cream

1 to 2 tablespoons heavy cream
(optional)

Mix the espresso, papaya, coconut, $\frac{1}{8}$ kiwi, and the ice cream in a blender for 15 to 20 seconds, or until smooth. Garnish with the remaining kiwi and pour the cream lightly on top, if desired.

Serves 1

Gourmet

Coffee

Drinks

with

Liquor

J ust as various flavors and spices can be added to your gourmet coffee drinks, so can a wide variety of liquors. The combinations are virtually endless, but among the most popular additions are rum, whiskey, and such liqueurs as brandy, cognac, crème de menthe, crème de cacao, amaretto, anisette, Irish cream, Kahlúa and Tia Maria, Cointreau and Grand Marnier, Galliano and Frangelico. Liquors such as these can be used in combination with each other—using either hot or cold brewed coffee or espresso—and they can also be added to a cup of coffee all by themselves. You may also wish to add a little bit of kirsch, vodka, tequila, gin, curaçao, crème de banana, cherry liqueur, calvados, Benedictine, Tuaca, Strega, Sambuca, or Drambuie to your coffee, depending on your taste. By all means experiment with the quantity and combination of liquors you use in each drink, as well as with the amount of coffee, milk, flavors, spices, and other ingredients that you wish to use. Who knows? You just might develop a few interesting concoctions of your own. The recipes in this chapter are for hot and cold potables made with regular brewed coffee or espresso. Enjoy!

Hot Drinks Made with Brewed Coffee

These drinks are made with freshly brewed coffee and should be served immediately.

Bailey's–Crème de Cacao Coffee

Whether you use Frangelico or amaretto, it will be a sweet, refreshing concoction that is sure to satisfy.

$1\frac{1}{2}$ tablespoons Bailey's
  Original Irish Cream
$1\frac{1}{2}$ tablespoons crème de
  cacao
$\frac{1}{4}$ teaspoon Frangelico

$\frac{3}{4}$ cup coffee
$\frac{1}{4}$ cup heavy cream,
  whipped
Ground cinnamon

Combine the Bailey's, crème de cacao, and Frangelico in a glass and add the coffee. Top with whipped cream and a dash of cinnamon.

Serves 1

Variation: Substitute $\frac{1}{4}$ teaspoon amaretto for the Frangelico. Proceed as directed above.

Café Brûlot

This is a fun drink for a winter afternoon because the process of making it is as warming as drinking the concoction itself.

1½ ounces brandy or cognac

1 teaspoon white or brown sugar

2 whole cloves

1 cinnamon stick

1 strip orange peel

1 strip lemon peel

¾ cup coffee

1 teaspoon Cointreau or Grand Marnier (optional)

Place all the ingredients except the coffee and Cointreau in a saucepan and warm over low heat for 1 to 2 minutes, stirring occasionally. Add the coffee and stir into the mixture. Strain into a cup. Add the Cointreau, if desired.

Serves 1

Kahlúa—Crème de Menthe Coffee

The taste of the coffee liqueur comes through in this peppermint-flavored drink.

2 tablespoons Kahlúa

2 tablespoons crème de menthe

¾ cup coffee

¼ cup heavy cream, whipped

Sweetened chocolate powder

Mix the Kahlúa and crème de menthe in a glass. Add the coffee and top with whipped cream and chocolate powder.

Serves 1

Variation: For a Kahlúa–Crème de Cacao Coffee, omit the crème de menthe and substitute 2 tablespoons crème de cacao. Proceed as directed above.

Kahlúa–Grand Marnier Coffee

This orangy drink retains the creamy coffee taste of the Bailey's and the Kahlúa.

1½ teaspoons Kahlúa	¾ cup coffee
1½ teaspoons Grand Marnier	¼ cup heavy cream, whipped
1½ teaspoons Bailey's Original Irish Cream	Grated orange peel, for garnish
1½ teaspoons Frangelico	

Combine the Kahlúa, Grand Marnier, Bailey's, and Frangelico in a glass. Add the coffee and top with whipped cream. Garnish with orange peel.

Serves 1

Irish Coffee

This is a classic drink, popular throughout the world—and for good reason!

1 teaspoon sugar
2 tablespoons Irish whiskey
⅔ cup coffee

¼ cup heavy cream, lightly whipped

Place the sugar and whiskey in glass, add the coffee, and stir. Top with lightly whipped cream.

Serves 1

Kioki Coffee

The blend of brandy and Kahlúa gives this drink a unique taste. The whipped cream makes it even more special.

2 tablespoons Kahlúa
1 tablespoon brandy
1 cup coffee

¼ cup heavy cream, whipped

Pour the Kahlúa and brandy into a mug. Add the coffee and top with whipped cream.

Serves 1

Variation: Instead of 2 tablespoons Kahlúa, use 1 tablespoon Kahlúa and 1 tablespoon crème de cacao. Proceed as directed above.

Hot Drinks Made with Espresso

The following drinks are made with fresh espresso that is still hot. Serve immediately.

Espresso Anisette: A single espresso with 1 teaspoon of anisette added. Serve with a small slice of lemon peel.

Espresso Galliano: A single espresso with 1 teaspoon of Galliano added. Serve with a small slice of lemon peel.

Espresso Kahlúa: A single espresso with 1 teaspoon of Kahlúa added and topped with foam from steamed milk.

Espresso Rum: A single espresso with 1 teaspoon of rum added. Top with whipped cream and a dash of ground cinnamon.

Espresso Whiskey: A single espresso with ½ teaspoon of Irish whiskey added. Top with whipped cream.

Caffè Corretto: A single espresso with ½ teaspoon of grappa added.

Cappuccino Calypso

The coffee-rum taste of this drink is delicious.

Single espresso
(page 40)
2 tablespoons Tia Maria

1½ teaspoons rum
3 ounces milk, steamed

Mix all the ingredients except the milk in a glass. Add 1½ ounces steamed milk and 1½ ounces milk foam.

Serves 1

Amaretto-Rum Cappuccino

The almond-cream taste of this drink is sure to satisfy.

Single espresso
(page 40)
1½ teaspoons amaretto
1½ teaspoons rum
1½ teaspoons crème de cacao

3 ounces milk, steamed
¼ cup heavy cream, whipped
Sliced almonds, for garnish

Mix the espresso, amaretto, rum, and crème de cacao in a glass. Add 1½ ounces steamed milk and 1½ ounces milk foam. Top with whipped cream and garnish with almond slices.

Serves 1

Brandy-Rum Mochaccino

This drink's chocolate-brandy-rum combination makes it a special one for chocolate lovers.

Single espresso
(page 40)
1½ teaspoons brandy
1½ teaspoons rum
1½ teaspoons crème de cacao
1 tablespoon chocolate syrup

3 ounces milk, steamed
¼ cup heavy cream, whipped
Ground cinnamon
Ground nutmeg
Thin wafer, for garnish

Mix the espresso, brandy, rum, crème de cacao, and chocolate syrup in a glass. Add 1½ ounces steamed milk and 1½ ounces milk foam. Top with whipped cream, sprinkle with cinnamon and nutmeg, and garnish with a wafer.

Serves 1

Grasshopper Cappuccino

This minty drink is also excellent poured over ice.

*Single espresso
(page 40)*

*1½ teaspoons crème de
menthe*

*1½ teaspoons crème de
cacao*

3 ounces milk, steamed

*¼ cup heavy cream,
whipped*

*Sweetened chocolate
powder*

*Fresh mint sprig, for
garnish*

Mix the espresso, crème de menthe, and crème de cacao in a glass. Add 1½ ounces steamed milk and 1½ ounces milk foam. Top with whipped cream and chocolate powder and garnish with a fresh mint sprig.

Serves 1

Variation: For a Grasshopper Mochaccino, stir 1 teaspoon chocolate syrup into the milk before steaming it or stir the syrup into the espresso before mixing. Proceed as directed above.

Cold Drinks Made with Brewed Coffee

The following drinks are made with cold coffee. Although they are the perfect antidote to a hot summer day, they are delicious any time of the year.

Iced Amaretto–Brandy Coffee

The almond and brandy tastes in this drink complement each other perfectly.

1 ounce amaretto

1 tablespoon brandy

$\frac{3}{4}$ cup coffee

Ice cubes

$\frac{1}{4}$ cup heavy cream, whipped

Sliced almonds, for garnish

Add the amaretto and brandy to the coffee. Pour over ice, top with whipped cream, and garnish with sliced almonds.

Serves 1

Blended Chocolate-Brandy Coffee

Brandy and chocolate combine beautifully to make this a great drink for a warm summer afternoon.

$\frac{1}{2}$ cup coffee
$\frac{1}{2}$ cup milk
2 tablespoons brandy

2 tablespoons chocolate syrup
Ice cubes

Mix all the ingredients together in a blender for 15 to 20 seconds, or until frothy. Pour over ice in a tall glass.

Serves 1

Coffee-Rum Blended

Coffee and rum combine superbly in this smooth-textured cooler.

$\frac{1}{4}$ cup coffee
$\frac{1}{4}$ cup milk
$1\frac{1}{2}$ tablespoons rum

$1\frac{1}{2}$ tablespoons crème de cacao
1 scoop coffee ice cream

Mix all the ingredients together in a blender for 15 to 20 seconds, or until smooth.

Serves 1

Coffee Alexander

The tastes of Kahlúa, amaretto, and chocolate combine to give this drink a real punch.

¾ cup coffee
1½ tablespoons Kahlúa
1½ tablespoons amaretto
2 scoops chocolate ice cream

Ice cubes
½ cup heavy cream, whipped
Sweetened chocolate powder

Mix the coffee, Kahlúa, amaretto, and ice cream in a blender for 15 to 20 seconds, or until smooth. Pour over ice and top with whipped cream and chocolate powder.

Serves 2

Variation: Substitute 2 scoops of vanilla ice cream for the chocolate. Proceed as directed above, topping with a dash of ground nutmeg or cinnamon instead of sweetened chocolate powder.

Cold Drinks Made with Espresso

Unless otherwise specified, the following drinks are made with freshly made espresso and served immediately.

Kahlúa-Rum Chocolate Espresso Float

This cool, sweet treat will melt in your mouth!

Double espresso, cold (page 40)
1 teaspoon Kahlúa
1 teaspoon rum

1 scoop chocolate ice cream
¼ cup heavy cream, whipped
Sweetened chocolate powder

Combine the espresso, Kahlúa, and rum in a glass. Add the ice cream and top with whipped cream and chocolate powder.

Serves 1

Kahlúa–Crème de Cacao Iced Cappuccino

This sweet, creamy concoction is sure to perk you up on a warm day.

Single espresso
(page 40)
3 ounces milk
1½ teaspoons Kahlúa
1½ teaspoons crème de cacao

Ice cubes
¼ cup heavy cream, whipped
Ground cinnamon or sweetened chocolate powder

Mix the espresso, milk, Kahlúa, and crème de cacao together and pour over ice. Top with whipped cream and cinnamon or chocolate powder.

Serves 1

Cocoa-Mint Espresso Shake

The cocoa-mint combination, mixed with the espresso and vanilla ice cream, makes for a great-tasting pick-me-up.

Single espresso (page 40)
1 teaspoon crème de cacao

¼ teaspoon crème de menthe
1 scoop vanilla ice cream

Mix all the ingredients together in a blender for 15 to 20 seconds, or until smooth.

Serves 1

Iced Brandy–Cointreau Espresso

This drink is just as good using hot espresso.

Double espresso, cold
(page 40)
1 teaspoon brandy
1 teaspoon Cointreau
Ice cubes

¼ cup heavy cream, whipped
Grated orange peel, for
garnish

Combine the espresso, brandy, and Cointreau and pour over ice. Top with whipped cream and garnish with grated orange peel.

Serves 1

Variation: For an Iced Brandy–Crème de Cacao Espresso, omit the Cointreau and substitute 1 teaspoon crème de cacao. Garnish with sweetened chocolate powder instead of grated orange peel.

MAKING YOUR OWN GOURMET TEA DRINKS

To Jane Jordan Browne

Acknowledgments

This is a special acknowledgment for all of the great people at Crown Publishers. No writer could ask for a better team, from editing to production to sales. I would especially like to thank Betty A. Prashker and Michelle Sidrane for their continued support. Thanks as well to Nancy Maloney, Pam Romano, and Robin Strashun for their fine efforts on my behalf. As always, I would like to thank my editor, Brandt Aymar, for his great advice and my literary agent, Jane Jordan Browne, for her continued support. Special thanks to my parents for the use of their great kitchen while I tested these recipes!

Contents

Introduction

People have been drinking tea for thousands of years. Discovered in ancient China, this beverage spread around the world over the centuries, first to Japan, then to Europe and America. • Tea has affected every culture in which it has been introduced, from the Japanese tea ceremony to the British custom of afternoon tea. • In his classic work, The Book of Tea, Kakuzo Okakura states: "The afternoon tea is now an important function in Western society. In the delicate clatter of trays and saucers, in the soft rustle of feminine hospitality, in

the common catechism about cream and sugar, we know that the Worship of Tea is established beyond question." • Even though Okakura wrote those words in 1906, the spirit of tea not only has continued to flourish over the years, but is currently enjoying a new burst of popularity. • Today, educated tea drinkers ask their specialty tea shop for black teas with names like Assam, Darjeeling, Lapsang Souchong, and Yunnan; green teas called

Gunpowder and Gyokuro; scented teas such as Earl Grey and Jasmine; flavored black teas like Raspberry, Peach, and Mango; herbal teas such as Mint and Chamomile, as well as flavored herbal teas such as Almond,

 Cinnamon, and Lemon. • And in tearooms, restaurants, and hotels across the country, afternoon tea, at which pots of gourmet tea such as Apricot, Black Currant, Russian Caravan, Orange-and-Spice, and Vanilla tea are served alongside such standards

as English and Irish Breakfast tea, has become a popular pastime. • With this book, you will be able to bring the taste (and, I hope, the spirit) of your local tearoom right into your own home. You will learn how to make the best cup of tea possible, and you will be introduced to some creative ways of serving your tea drinks—both hot and cold. • In addition to the recipes included here, feel free to create your own gourmet tea drinks with whichever teas and other ingredients you prefer, depending on your taste. Who knows? You might come up with a few classic tea drinks of your own. • Happy brewing!

The Various Types of Tea
You Can Use

All black, green, and oolong tea (as opposed to herb tea) comes from one plant—*Camellia sinensis,* an evergreen shrub that thrives in warm, rainy climates in various parts of the world. Most of the world's tea is produced and manufactured in China, India, Sri Lanka (formerly Ceylon), Japan, and Taiwan (formerly Formosa)—although tea is also grown in such diverse places as Indonesia, Kenya, Argentina, and Russia.

Depending on where in the world it is grown, the specific variety (or subspecies) of *Camellia sinensis* that it is, and how it is manufactured, tea from different regions (and carrying different names) will feature its own characteristic taste.

For instance, Lapsang Souchong black tea from China features a smoky, full-bodied taste, while Ceylon black tea offers a more subtle, middle-of-the-road taste sensation to the drinker.

Darjeeling black tea from India has its own distinctive, delicate taste, which is known the world over, while Assam black tea, also from India, features a stronger, heavier taste.

In addition to single varieties of black tea, a number of black tea blends are popular in the tea-drinking world: English Breakfast tea is usually a blend of Ceylon and Assam teas; Irish Breakfast tea, a blend of Assam teas, has a stronger taste; Russian Caravan tea, a blend of China black and oolong teas, features the smoky taste of Lapsang Souchong; and Earl Grey tea is a blend of black teas that is scented with oil of bergamot.

Any of these black tea varieties or black tea blends (and others like them) can be used in the gourmet tea drink recipes that follow, depending on your taste.

When black tea is manufactured, it is allowed to ferment (or oxidize) before it is fired (i.e., dried by hot air); hence its black color.

Green tea is not allowed to ferment before it is fired, so it remains green. Oolong tea is allowed to partially ferment before it is fired, so its color and taste lie somewhere between that of black and green tea. Green tea and oolong tea are usually served as a single variety and are not blended the way black tea is.

Flavored (or scented) black teas have become increasingly popular in recent years, and it is now not uncommon for a gourmet tea connoisseur to order a few ounces of some black currant– or strawberry-flavored tea along with his or her Darjeeling or Ceylon tea.

Some flavored teas, such as Orange-and-Spice tea, actually have small pieces of orange peel, cinnamon, and cloves mixed in with the black tea, while others, such as Vanilla tea, actually have small pieces of vanilla bean added to them.

Sometimes pieces of dried fruit such as mango and apple are added to the tea, and in some cases, essential oils are used to flavor teas.

Jasmine tea is made by mixing green, oolong, or pouchong tea (which is slightly less fermented than oolong tea) with fresh jasmine petals during the manufacturing process, so that the tea leaves actually pick up the scent of the flowers. The same process is used with rose petals and black tea when making Rose tea. Although the petals with these teas often remain in the loose tea, they have little or no effect on the taste.

Most unflavored and flavored black teas are available in decaffeinated form. Green tea and oolong tea contain considerably less caffeine than black tea, so these types of tea are not available in decaffeinated form.

Herb teas (also called infusions or tisanes) consist of the flowers and leaves of plants other than *Camellia sinensis.* They are generally caffeine-free and are usually used in their dried form. Fresh herbs and flowers, when available, can also be used for making herb tea. Sometimes the stems, seeds, roots, and bark of various plants are also used in herb teas.

Some of the most popular herb teas include Mint, Chamomile, Rose Hips, and Hibiscus. In addition, many commercially available herb teas are flavored with pieces of fruit and various spices, as well as essential oils.

Herb teas can be blended together (as are black teas) before brewing, and they can also be grown in your garden, if you want to use them in their fresh form or dry them yourself for later use. You can also brew your herb teas separately and then mix them together in liquid form. (This is generally not done with black teas.)

Thai tea is a special type of loose tea that is flavored with star anise. It is used for making Thai Iced Tea (page 65).

In general, black, green, oolong, and herbal gourmet teas are commercially available at specialty tea shops (or tearooms), by mail order from gourmet tea suppliers, and on your local supermarket shelves. Many gourmet coffee retailers also offer full lines of tea, both for in-store purchases and by mail. Thai tea is generally available at Thai food markets across the country.

A Word About Equipment

The equipment that you will need for making a great cup of gourmet tea is really very simple and has remained virtually unchanged for hundreds, if not thousands, of years.

First, you will need a teapot—ceramic or glass is best. You may want to have both a 2-cup teapot and a 4-cup teapot on hand (or even a 6-cup teapot), depending on how much tea you plan to make at any given time. There are even 1-cup teapots available that are modeled after the traditional Chinese teapots designed for individual servings.

Some teapots come with their own built-in infusers (i.e., perforated baskets for holding the loose tea). If your teapot does not have a built-in infuser, you can use either a metal ball or spoon infuser to hold the loose tea while it is brewing in the teapot.

Be sure to fill the infuser only halfway up with the loose tea, as tea leaves expand when wet and will quickly fill up the infuser and prevent the easy flow of water through the leaves. If you want to make a larger batch of tea, simply use two half-filled infusers.

Another type of infuser that is quite effective consists of a paper filter (much like a large, open tea bag) that fits around the outside of a plastic ring with a handle. Fill the bag with tea and place the handle across the top of your teapot so the homemade tea bag hangs into the teapot and acts as a built-in infuser.

If you choose not to use an infuser and just place the loose tea in your teapot, you will need a strainer to catch the leaves that come out of the spout when you pour the tea. You can either place the strainer over your teacup or attach a strainer to the spout of the teapot.

For making Thai Iced Tea (page 65), you will need a Thai tea strainer, which consists of a cloth bag about one foot long that is attached to a metal ring. Thai tea strainers are generally available at Thai food markets across the country. (You can also use your own cloth bag.)

Two other pieces of equipment are important when it comes to making the best gourmet tea possible: an opaque, airtight container (i.e., a tin or tea caddy) for storing your tea and a tea cozy (a padded covering for your teapot that will keep the tea hot). Be sure to remove the tea leaves before placing the cozy on the teapot or your tea will overbrew.

In general, loose tea can be stored in a tea tin for six months to a year before losing some of its flavor. (Flavored teas will lose their flavor more quickly than unflavored teas.) Keep the tin in a cool, dark, dry place. Do not put it in the refrigerator, as moisture from the refrigerator will quickly ruin your tea.

How to Make the Best Cup
of Hot Tea

Here are a few tips for making the best cup of hot tea possible with the equipment that you have. The following instructions apply to black, green, and oolong tea, as well as to fresh and dried herb teas, unless otherwise specified. (Since characteristics of herb teas vary so much, feel free to use more or less herb tea and shorter or longer brewing times than those specified here, depending on your taste.)

1. Always use fresh, cold water; your cup of tea is only as good as the water that is used to make it.

2. In general, you should use 1 teaspoon of loose tea (or 1 tea bag) for every 6 ounces of water that you use. Some people like to add an extra teaspoon of loose tea (or 1 extra tea bag) "for the pot" as well. It is up to you.

3. Preheat the teapot by rinsing it out with hot water, then place the tea in the teapot.

4. Bring the water to a full, rolling boil and then pour the water into the teapot. (For green tea, use water that is just off the boil.)

5. Brew the tea for 3 to 5 minutes, depending on your taste. (If you are using tea bags, you may want to brew the tea for a little shorter time than loose tea, as the larger surface area of finely chopped tea in

bags causes its flavor to be extracted more rapidly than loose tea, which generally has larger leaves.) Then remove the loose tea or tea bags from the teapot, or pour the tea through a strainer.

6. Always serve your tea immediately after you make it to retain both the heat and the freshness of the tea.

7. Be sure to clean your teapot, kettle, and all of your other tea-making equipment regularly so that tea residues or mineral deposits do not build up and ruin future cups of tea.

Making Iced Tea

There are a number of ways to make iced tea.

One method involves brewing the tea as you normally would with hot water, only use 1½ to 2 times the amount of loose tea or tea bags as normal to account for the dilution factor of ice cubes. Pour the tea over ice immediately or after the tea has cooled to room temperature.

The *sun tea method* involves placing 1½ to 2 times the normal amount of loose tea or tea bags in a glass container along with the normal amount of cold water that you would use for that batch of tea. Loosely cap the container and place it in the sun for 2 to 4 hours, depending on your taste. Then remove the loose tea or tea bags from the container, or pour the tea through a strainer. Pour over ice.

The *cold-water method* of making iced tea involves placing 1½ to 2 times the normal amount of loose tea or tea bags in a container along with the normal amount of cold water that you would use for that batch of tea. Then place the container in the refrigerator for 6 to 8 hours, depending on your taste. Remove the loose tea or tea bags from the container, or pour the tea through a strainer. Pour over ice.

In general, iced tea can be stored in the refrigerator for a few days, but it is always best to make it as fresh as possible.

If you prepare your iced tea using hot water, the tea can become cloudy when chilled, depending on the type of tea that you use. (This does not affect the taste at all!) In order to make the tea more clear, simply add a little bit of boiling water to the tea and stir it around. Iced tea that is made with the sun tea or cold-water method will remain clear even when refrigerated.

A Note on Ingredients

1. When not otherwise specified, regular granulated sugar (or other sweeteners, such as honey and brown sugar) can be added to any of these drinks, depending on your taste. Many of the drinks taste fine without any sugar at all.

2. I use regular granulated sugar, but an equal amount of honey can be used as well.

3. I use whole milk, but low-fat or even nonfat milk can also be used, depending on your taste.

4. It is always best to use fresh whipped cream—generally about ¼ cup per drink.

5. I use chocolate syrup, but an equal amount of sweetened chocolate powder can be used as well.

6. I use unsweetened cranberry juice, which is available at most health food stores.

7. I use bottled or canned apricot nectar, which contains corn syrup. This will make the drink sweeter than if you use unsweetened apricot nectar, from freshly juiced apricots.

8. In the recipes using grape juice, I usually suggest using either white or Concord grape juice, but feel free to use whichever type tastes best to you.

9. When used as garnishes, orange, lemon, lime, apple, and peach slices may be peeled or not. It is up to you. Kiwifruit and pineapple slices should be peeled.

10. Nectarine slices can be substituted for peach slices.

11. Unless otherwise specified, I use jam, but an equal amount of jelly or preserves can also be used.

12. I use cinnamon sticks, but ⅛ teaspoon of ground cinnamon can be used instead of a cinnamon stick (except as a garnish).

13. Orange-flavored herb tea may also be called Orange-and-Spice herb tea. Either will do.

14. If you wish to make more (or fewer) servings of these drinks, simply multiply (or divide) the amount of each ingredient to provide for the number of servings that you wish to make.

Hot *Drinks* Made *with* Black *Tea*

Unless otherwise specified, all of the drinks in this chapter are made with freshly brewed tea that is still hot, and should be served immediately.

Pineapple Tea

This drink also tastes great when poured over ice—and the pineapple slices are a sweet treat whether hot or cold!

1½ cups black tea
½ cup pineapple juice

2 cinnamon sticks
Pineapple slices, for garnish

110

Combine the tea, pineapple juice, and cinnamon sticks in a saucepan and simmer over low heat for 1 to 2 minutes, stirring occasionally. Remove the cinnamon sticks and pour the mixture into 2 cups. Garnish with fresh slices of pineapple.

Serves 2

Raspberry Tea

What a delight this drink is! You get the great taste of raspberries from three ingredients—and that is before you add the whipped cream and mint!

1 tablespoon fresh raspberries	Fresh mint sprig, for
¾ cup raspberry-flavored	garnish
black tea	Sugar to taste (optional)
1 teaspoon raspberry jam	Whipped cream (optional)

Place the raspberries at the bottom of a cup and pour the tea over the raspberries. Stir in the jam and garnish with a fresh mint sprig. Add the sugar and top with the whipped cream, if desired.

Serves 1

Variations: For a Strawberry Tea, substitute 1 tablespoon sliced fresh strawberries, ¾ cup strawberry-flavored black tea, and 1 teaspoon strawberry jam for the raspberries, raspberry-flavored black tea, and raspberry jam. Proceed as directed above.

For a Peach Tea, substitute 1 tablespoon peeled and sliced fresh peaches, ¾ cup peach-flavored black tea, and 1 teaspoon peach jam for the raspberries, raspberry-flavored black tea, and raspberry jam. Proceed as directed above.

Cranapple Tea

The hot apple slices in this drink are a great treat—and they also serve as a natural sweetener.

2 cups black tea
½ cup cranberry juice
1½ cups apple juice
2 cinnamon sticks

4 whole cloves
Sugar to taste (optional)
Apple slices, for garnish

Combine the tea, juices, cinnamon sticks, and cloves in a saucepan and simmer over low heat for 3 to 4 minutes, stirring occasionally. Remove the spices and pour the mixture into 4 cups. Add sugar to each individual cup, if desired, and garnish with a slice of apple.

Serves 4

Maple Tea

Bring the taste of Vermont to your tea with the maple syrup, and add just the right spicy touch with the cinnamon.

¾ cup black tea
1 tablespoon maple syrup
¼ cup heavy cream, whipped

Ground cinnamon, for garnish

Pour the tea into a cup. Stir the maple syrup into the tea, top with whipped cream, and sprinkle with cinnamon.

Serves 1

Apricot Tea

The apricot nectar enhances the taste of this drink, which is made with one of the most popular of the flavored gourmet teas.

1 cup apricot nectar
2 cinnamon sticks
4 small strips of orange peel
4 small strips of lemon peel

3 cups apricot-flavored
black tea
Brown sugar to taste
(optional)

Combine the apricot nectar, cinnamon sticks, orange peel, and lemon peel in a saucepan and simmer over low heat for 1 to 2 minutes, stirring occasionally. Add the tea and stir to mix all the ingredients together. Remove the cinnamon sticks and the orange and lemon peel and pour 6 ounces of the mixture into each of 4 cups. Add the brown sugar, if desired.

Serves 4

Brown Sugar Tea

Brown sugar, cinnamon, and whipped cream turn regular black tea into a simple yet special treat.

½ cup milk
2 tablespoons brown sugar
1 cinnamon stick
1½ cups black tea

½ cup heavy cream, whipped
Ground cinnamon, for garnish

Combine the milk, brown sugar, and cinnamon stick in a saucepan and simmer over low heat for 1 to 2 minutes, stirring occasionally. Add the tea and stir so that all of the ingredients are mixed together. Pour this mixture into 2 cups, top with whipped cream, and sprinkle with cinnamon.

Serves 2

Cardamom Tea

Whether you serve this drink with milk, sugar, or all by itself, the exotic taste of cardamom will mix well with the distinctive taste of Darjeeling tea.

2 teaspoons loose
Darjeeling tea
¼ teaspoon cardamom seeds

1½ cups water
Milk to taste (optional)
Sugar to taste (optional)

Place the tea in a teapot. Combine the cardamom seeds and the water in a saucepan and simmer over low heat for 3 to 5 minutes, stirring occasionally. Pour this water into the teapot and let the tea steep for 3 to 5 minutes, depending on your taste. Strain into 2 cups and add milk or sugar, if desired.

Serves 2

Cinnamon Tea

The great taste of cinnamon is featured in this drink, from top to bottom—literally!

115

1 teaspoon loose cinnamon-flavored black tea, or
1 tea bag
1 cinnamon stick
³⁄₄ cup water

¹⁄₄ cup milk
1 teaspoon sugar
¹⁄₄ cup heavy cream, whipped
Ground cinnamon, for garnish

Place the tea and the cinnamon stick in a teapot, bring the water to a boil, and pour the water into the teapot. Let the tea steep for 3 to 5 minutes, depending on your taste, and then strain (or pour) the tea into a cup. Stir in the milk and sugar and top with the whipped cream. Sprinkle with the cinnamon.

Serves 1

Ginger Tea

The taste of ginger adds a spicy accent to black tea, and the lemon adds a zesty tang.

⅛ teaspoon ground ginger (or ½ teaspoon peeled and sliced fresh ginger)
2 teaspoons loose black tea

1½ cups water
2 teaspoons sugar
Lemon peel or fresh mint sprigs, for garnish

Place the ginger at the bottom of the teapot along with the tea. Bring the water to a boil and pour the water into the teapot. Let the tea steep for 3 to 5 minutes, depending on your taste. Pour 6 ounces of the tea into each of 2 cups. Add 1 teaspoon of sugar to each cup and garnish with small strips of lemon peel or fresh mint sprigs.

Serves 2

Spiced Cider Tea

What a delightful drink—like a tea cider! Enjoy this drink on a crisp autumn day as the leaves are falling—or anytime else, for that matter.

½ cup apple cider
1 cinnamon stick
2 whole cloves

⅛ teaspoon ground allspice
½ cup black tea

Combine the cider, cinnamon stick, cloves, and allspice in a saucepan and simmer over low heat for 1 to 2 minutes, stirring occasionally. Pour the tea into the cider mixture and stir all of the ingredients together. Strain into a mug.

Serves 1

Orange-and-Spice Tea

This milky elixir tastes like ambrosia—especially when sugar is added.

½ cup milk
1 cinnamon stick
2 whole cloves
⅛ teaspoon ground allspice
⅛ teaspoon ground nutmeg

½ cup orange-and-spice–
flavored black tea
Sugar to taste (optional)
Ground nutmeg, for
garnish (optional)

Combine the milk, cinnamon stick, cloves, allspice, and nutmeg in a saucepan and simmer over low heat for 1 to 2 minutes, stirring occasionally. Pour the tea into the saucepan and stir all of the ingredients until they are mixed together. Strain this mixture into a cup. If desired, add sugar and top with ground nutmeg.

Serves 1

Ice Cream Tea

The ice cream melts quickly, adding flavor to this drink.

¾ cup black tea

1 scoop vanilla or chocolate
ice cream

Pour the tea into a cup. Add the ice cream.

Serves 1

Mint Jelly Tea

The smoky taste of the Russian Caravan tea mixes well with the mint jelly for an exotic yet earthy drink. As a special treat, eat bits of the mint jelly as you enjoy this drink.

2 teaspoons mint jelly, or
to taste

1½ cups Russian Caravan or
another black tea

Place 1 teaspoon of jelly (or more, depending on your taste) at the bottom of each cup. Pour 6 ounces of tea into each cup and stir to the desired consistency. (You may wish to save the jelly at the bottom of the cup as a treat.)

Serves 2

Variations: Substitute orange marmalade or strawberry, cherry, raspberry, or apricot jam for the mint jelly. Proceed as directed above.

Gunpowder-Mint Tea

The delicate taste of green tea is given a light, minty aftertaste in this delicious drink, which is a traditional favorite in Morocco.

> *1 teaspoon loose Gunpowder green tea, or 1 tea bag*
> *⅛ teaspoon mint extract, or 1 teaspoon fresh or dried mint leaves*
>
> *1 teaspoon sugar (optional)*
> *¾ cup water*
> *Fresh mint sprig, for garnish*

Place the tea, mint extract or mint leaves, and sugar, if desired, in a teapot. Heat the water to a boil and pour the water into the teapot. Let the tea brew for 3 to 5 minutes, depending on your taste. Strain or pour the tea into a cup. Garnish with a fresh mint sprig.

Serves 1

NOTE: You can also mix fresh or dried mint leaves in with the Gunpowder tea before brewing—½ teaspoon of each works best. Then omit the mint extract from the recipe.

Spiced Jasmine Tea

The addition of the cinnamon stick and cloves brings some new flavors to an already flavorful tea.

> ½ cup milk
> 1 cinnamon stick
> 4 whole cloves
>
> 1½ cups jasmine tea
> Sugar to taste (optional)

Combine the milk, cinnamon stick, and cloves in a saucepan and simmer over low heat for 1 to 2 minutes, stirring occasionally. Pour the tea into the saucepan and stir to mix all the ingredients together. Remove the cinnamon stick and cloves and pour the tea into 2 cups. Add sugar, if desired.

Serves 2

Rose Black Tea

Add the flavor of rose petals to your black tea with this drink.

> 1 teaspoon loose black tea, or
>   1 tea bag
> ½ teaspoon dried rose petals,
>   or to taste
>
> ¾ cup water
> Sugar to taste (optional)

Place the tea and the rose petals at the bottom of the teapot. Boil the water and pour the water into the teapot. Let the tea brew for 3 to 5 minutes, depending on your taste. Strain into a cup and add sugar, if desired.

Serves 1

Mocha Tea

The chocolate and the whipped cream enhance the taste of the tea beautifully in this drink.

2 tablespoons chocolate syrup
$\frac{1}{3}$ cup milk
$\frac{2}{3}$ cup black tea

$\frac{1}{4}$ cup heavy cream, whipped
Sweetened chocolate powder

Stir the chocolate syrup into the milk in a saucepan over low heat for 1 to 2 minutes, or until hot (do not boil). Add the tea and stir so that all of the ingredients are mixed together. Pour this mixture into a cup, top with whipped cream, and sprinkle with chocolate powder.

Serves 1

Tea Grog

If you want an extra taste of cinnamon in your drink, use a cinnamon-flavored black tea or a cinnamon-flavored herb tea.

2 tablespoons butter
1 cup brown sugar
⅛ teaspoon ground allspice
⅛ teaspoon ground cinnamon
⅛ teaspoon ground nutmeg
⅛ teaspoon ground cloves
12 small strips of orange peel

12 small strips of lemon peel
9 cups black tea
   Milk or cream to taste
   (optional)
1½ teaspoons rum extract
   (optional)

Melt the butter in a saucepan over low heat. Stir in the brown sugar, allspice, cinnamon, nutmeg, and cloves and allow the mixture to cool. Store in a sealed container in the refrigerator.

To serve, combine in each cup 1 teaspoon of the grog mixture, 1 strip of orange peel, and 1 strip of lemon peel. Add 6 ounces of tea and stir. You can also add milk or cream or ⅛ teaspoon rum extract to each cup of grog, if desired.

Serves 12

Variation: Omit the allspice and cinnamon and double the amount of ground nutmeg and cloves. Proceed as directed above.

Chai I

This traditional Indian spiced tea is as much fun to make as it is to drink—and it is quick!

2 cups water
2 teaspoons loose black tea
(preferably Indian)
1/4 teaspoon tea masala
2 cardamom pods

2 teaspoons sugar
1/2 cup milk
1 tablespoon peeled and sliced
fresh ginger

Combine the water, tea, masala, cardamom, and 1 teaspoon of the sugar in a large saucepan and simmer over low heat for 5 minutes. Add the milk and the rest of the sugar. Add the ginger 1 to 2 minutes after that, or when the mixture is back to a simmer. Wait for 15 to 30 seconds and then strain the tea into 2 cups.

Serves 2

NOTE: Tea masala is a premade spice mixture of ground black pepper, ground cardamom, ground cloves, and ground cinnamon. It is available at most Indian food markets; you can also create your own, depending on your taste.

Variation: To make Chai I without milk and sugar, combine the water, tea, masala, and cardamom in a large saucepan and simmer over low heat for 5 minutes. Add the ginger, wait 15 to 30 seconds, and then strain the tea into 2 cups.

Chai II

If you want to make your own *chai* from scratch, just use your own spice mixture instead of a commercially available tea masala. Please feel free to add more or fewer spices to this recipe, depending on your taste.

2 cups water
2 teaspoons loose black tea
  (preferably Indian)
2 cardamom pods
1 cinnamon stick
2 whole cloves

2 teaspoons sugar
2 black peppercorns
  (optional)
½ cup milk
1 tablespoon peeled and sliced
  fresh ginger

Combine the water, tea, cardamom, cinnamon stick, cloves, 1 teaspoon of the sugar, and the peppercorns, if desired, in a large saucepan and simmer over low heat for 5 minutes. Add the milk and the rest of the sugar. Add the ginger 1 to 2 minutes after that, or when the mixture is back to a simmer. Wait for 15 to 30 seconds and then strain the tea into 2 cups.

Serves 2

Variation: To make Chai II without milk and sugar, combine the water, tea, cardamom, cinnamon stick, cloves, and peppercorns, if desired, in a large saucepan and simmer over low heat for 5 minutes. Add the ginger, wait 15 to 30 seconds, and then strain the tea into 2 cups.

Chai III

The taste of the fennel and the cardamom make a great combination in this drink.

2 cups water
2 teaspoons loose black tea
  (preferably Indian)
2 cardamom pods

¼ teaspoon fennel seeds
½ cup milk
  Sugar to taste (optional)

Combine the water, tea, cardamom, and fennel seeds in a large saucepan and simmer over low heat for 2 to 3 minutes. Add the milk and 1 to 2 minutes later, or when the mixture is back to a simmer, strain the tea into 2 cups. Add sugar, if desired.

Serves 2

Variation: To make Chai III without milk, combine the water, tea, cardamom, and fennel seeds in a large saucepan and simmer over low heat for 2 to 3 minutes. Strain the tea into 2 cups.

Hot
Drinks
Made
with
Herb
Tea

All of the drinks in this chapter are made with freshly brewed tea that is still hot, and should be served immediately.

Lemon-Mint Tea

The lemon slice is all the lemon you need in this drink to give a zesty accent to the mint tea.

1½ cups mint-flavored   2 teaspoons sugar
    herb tea   Lemon slices, for garnish

Pour the tea into 2 cups. Stir 1 teaspoon of sugar into each cup and garnish with slices of lemon.

Serves 2

Chamomile-Mint Tea

The refreshing mint taste complements the chamomile tea well—and the sugar and cream turn this drink into a real treat.

¾ cup chamomile tea   ¼ cup heavy cream, whipped
⅛ teaspoon mint extract   Fresh mint sprig, for
1 teaspoon sugar   garnish

Pour the tea into a cup. Stir in the mint extract and the sugar.
Top with whipped cream and garnish with a fresh mint sprig.

Serves 1

NOTE: You can also mix fresh or dried chamomile flowers
and mint leaves together before brewing—$\frac{1}{2}$ teaspoon of
each works best in $\frac{3}{4}$ cup water. Or you can simply add equal
amounts of brewed chamomile and mint tea together in the
same cup. Then omit the mint extract from the recipe.

Chocolate-Mint Tea Delight

This rich, smooth drink is a great dessert all by itself. Watch
the whipped cream settle on top and then slowly fall into the
drink. This one is a delight!

$\frac{3}{4}$ cup mint-flavored herb tea   *$\frac{1}{4}$ cup heavy cream, whipped*
2 tablespoons chocolate syrup   *Sweetened chocolate powder*

Pour the tea into a cup. Stir the chocolate syrup into the tea.
Top with whipped cream and sprinkle with chocolate
powder.

Serves 1

Lemon-Grape Tea

This drink is also delicious when served over ice, in which case you do not need to heat up the juice before mixing it with the tea.

½ cup white or Concord grape juice
1½ cups lemon-flavored herb tea

Lemon peel, for garnish (optional)

Bring the grape juice to a boil in a saucepan over low heat. Stir the tea into the juice and pour this mixture into 2 cups. Garnish with a small slice of lemon peel, if desired.

Serves 2

Variation: For a Lemon-Apple Tea, substitute ½ cup apple juice for the grape juice. Proceed as directed above.

Blackberry-Grape Tea

The cinnamon and allspice provide a delightful accent for this robust drink. You can also use blackberry-flavored black tea instead of blackberry-flavored herb tea with this drink.

½ cup Concord grape juice
1 cinnamon stick
⅛ teaspoon whole allspice

1 cup blackberry-flavored
herb tea

Combine the grape juice, cinnamon stick, and allspice in a saucepan and simmer over low heat for 1 to 2 minutes, stirring occasionally. Pour the tea into the saucepan and stir all the ingredients together. Remove the cinnamon stick and strain the tea into a large mug.

Serves 1

Orange-Apple Spiced Tea

The orange and apple slices float on the surface of this hot drink and get hot themselves—delicious!

½ cup apple juice
1 cinnamon stick
½ cup orange-flavored herb tea

Orange and apple slices, for garnish

Combine the apple juice and cinnamon stick in a saucepan and simmer over low heat for 1 to 2 minutes, stirring occasionally. Add the tea and stir all the ingredients together. Remove the cinnamon stick and pour the mixture into a mug and garnish with slices of orange and apple.

Serves 1

Cinnamon Tea Punch

The combination of the apple juice and the apricot nectar makes this drink special—along with the cinnamon, cinnamon, cinnamon!

1 cup apple juice
1 cup apricot nectar
2 cinnamon sticks
2 cups cinnamon-flavored
  herb tea

Ground cinnamon, for
garnish (optional)

Combine the juice, nectar, and cinnamon sticks in a saucepan and simmer over low heat for 1 to 2 minutes, stirring occasionally. Add the tea and stir to mix all the ingredients together. Remove the cinnamon sticks and pour the mixture into 4 mugs and sprinkle with ground cinnamon, if desired.

Serves 4

Hibiscus-Apple Tea

This healthy elixir combines the earthy taste of apples with the flowery taste of the hibiscus—and the tastes complement each other perfectly.

½ cup apple juice
1 cinnamon stick
½ cup hibiscus tea

Sugar to taste (optional)
Lemon peel, for garnish
(optional)

Combine the apple juice and cinnamon stick in a saucepan and simmer over low heat for 1 to 2 minutes, stirring occasionally. Pour the tea into the saucepan and stir all the ingredients together. Remove the cinnamon stick and pour the tea into a cup. Add sugar and garnish with a small slice of lemon peel, if desired.

Serves 1

Hibiscus-Honey Tea

The hibiscus, honey, and lemon peel blend together perfectly in this tangy yet sweet drink.

1 teaspoon dried hibiscus
flowers, or 1 tea bag of
hibiscus tea
2 whole cloves

¾ cup water
1 teaspoon honey
Lemon peel, for garnish

Place the hibiscus flowers or tea bag and cloves at the bottom of a teapot. Heat the water to boiling and pour the water into the teapot. Let the tea brew for 3 to 5 minutes and then strain or pour the tea into a cup. Stir the honey into the tea and garnish with a small slice of lemon peel.

Serves 1

Cold
Drinks
Made
with
Black
Tea

Unless otherwise specified, all of the drinks in this section are made with cold brewed tea. In order to account for the dilution factor of ice cubes, you should brew the tea using 1½ to 2 times the amount of loose tea or tea bags as normal. Then store the tea in a sealed container in the refrigerator.

Orange-Apple Iced Tea

This delightful drink uses two of our favorite fruits, along with two of our favorite spices.

4 teaspoons loose orange-and-spice–flavored black tea, or 4 tea bags
1 cinnamon stick
4 whole cloves

1½ cups water
Ice cubes
¾ cup apple juice
Orange slices, for garnish

Place the tea, cinnamon stick, and cloves in a teapot. Bring the water to a boil, pour the water into the teapot, and let the tea brew for 3 to 5 minutes, depending on your taste. Chill the tea and pour 6 ounces of the tea over ice in 2 tall glasses. Pour 6 tablespoons of the apple juice into each glass and garnish with slices of orange.

Serves 2

Black Currant–Apple Iced Tea

The black currant and apple tastes complement each other well in this drink—and the apple and orange slices *look* good, too!

½ cup black currant–flavored black tea	Ice cubes
½ cup apple juice	Apple or orange slices, for garnish

Mix the tea and apple juice together and pour over ice in a tall glass. Garnish with apple or orange slices, depending on your taste.

Serves 1

139

Apricot Iced Tea

The apricot and cranberry tastes mix together well in this punchlike drink—and the orange slice adds just the sweet accent the drink needs.

¾ cup apricot-flavored
    black tea
2 tablespoons apricot nectar
2 tablespoons cranberry juice

Ice cubes
Sugar to taste
Orange slice, for garnish

Mix the tea, nectar, and juice together and pour over ice. Add sugar and garnish with a slice of orange.

Serves 1

Raspberry-Mint Iced Tea

Raspberry and mint provide a rich treat.

¾ cup raspberry-flavored
    black tea
Ice cubes
⅛ teaspoon mint extract

1 teaspoon sugar
¼ cup heavy cream, whipped
Fresh mint sprig, for
    garnish

Pour the tea over ice in a large glass. Stir in the mint extract and the sugar. Top with whipped cream and garnish with a fresh mint sprig.

Serves 1

Grape-Mint Iced Tea

The tastes of the mint and the grape go back and forth in this refreshing drink, which will cool you down on a hot summer day.

1 cup mint-flavored black tea
1 cup Concord grape juice
Ice cubes

Fresh mint sprigs, for garnish

Mix the tea and juice together and pour this mixture over ice in 2 large glasses. Garnish with fresh mint sprigs.

Serves 2

Cherry Iced Tea

This drink is like a cherry-flavored ice cream soda. You even get a real cherry with each serving!

½ cup cherry-flavored black tea	¼ cup cherry soda
Ice cubes	1 scoop vanilla ice cream
	Fresh cherry, for garnish

Pour the tea over ice in a tall glass. Add the cherry soda and ice cream. Garnish with a fresh cherry.

Serves 1

Peach Tea Punch

The apple and grape juices bring out the flavor of the tea in this drink. Enjoy it under an umbrella on a hot summer afternoon.

2 cups peach-flavored black tea	1 cup ginger ale
½ cup apple juice	Ice cubes
½ cup Concord or white grape juice	Fresh peach slices, for garnish

Mix the tea, juices, and ginger ale together in a pitcher and pour this mixture over ice in 4 tall glasses. Garnish with slices of fresh peach.

Serves 4

Lemon Tea Punch

For lemon lovers, this drink is a real treat!

1 cup lemon-flavored	*½ cup pineapple juice*
black tea	*½ cup lemon-lime soda*
Ice cubes	*Lemon slices, for garnish*

Pour the tea over ice in 2 tall glasses. Stir the juice and soda into the tea and garnish with slices of lemon.

Serves 2

Passion Fruit Tea Punch

The orange and lime slices add their own distinct flavors to the tea, while the kiwi and pineapple slices provide tropical fruit treats that you can enjoy while you are drinking this refresher.

*¾ cup passion fruit–flavored
    black tea
  Ice cubes
¼ cup carbonated water
  (optional)*

*Sugar to taste (optional)
Orange, lime, pineapple,
and kiwifruit slices, for
garnish*

Pour the tea over ice in a large glass. Add the carbonated water and sugar, if desired, and garnish with the slices of fruit.

Serves 1

Variation: For a Mango Tea Punch, substitute mango-flavored black tea for the passion fruit–flavored black tea. Proceed as directed above.

Tea Crush

The sweet-sour taste of the orange and lemon juices in this drink is a classic combination—and the orange and lemon slices add just the right touch. Serve this one right away, while it is still frothy.

¾ cup English Breakfast or
another black tea
1 tablespoon lemon juice
1 tablespoon orange juice
½ cup crushed ice

Sugar to taste
Ice cubes
Lemon and orange slices,
for garnish

Mix the tea, juices, crushed ice, and sugar in a blender for 15 to 20 seconds, or until smooth. Pour over ice in a tall glass and garnish with a slice of lemon and a slice of orange.

Serves 1

Banana Tea Blend

This drink is a great pick-me-up—like a snack. Serve it right away, while it is still frothy.

½ cup black tea	½ peeled and sliced banana
½ cup milk	Whipped cream (optional)

Mix all the ingredients except the whipped cream in a blender for 15 to 20 seconds, or until smooth. Top with whipped cream, if desired.

Serves 1

Variation: For a Banana-Chocolate Tea Blend, add 1 tablespoon chocolate syrup to the recipe. Proceed as directed above.

Strawberry Tea Shake

The flavor of the tea combines with the flavor of the ice cream to create a great summer afternoon treat.

¾ cup strawberry-flavored black tea	Sliced fresh strawberries, for garnish
2 scoops strawberry ice cream	Whipped cream (optional)
	Ice cubes (optional)

Mix the tea and the ice cream in a blender for 15 to 20 seconds, or until smooth. Pour into 2 tall glasses and garnish with sliced fresh strawberries. Top with whipped cream and pour over ice, if desired.

Serves 1

Variation: For a Peach Tea Shake, substitute peach-flavored black tea, peach ice cream, and slices of peeled fresh peach for the strawberry-flavored black tea, strawberry ice cream, and fresh strawberries. Proceed as directed above.

Vanilla Tea Shake

The nutmeg adds a great aftertaste to this drink and the whipped cream tops it off beautifully. Serve this one right away, before it has time to settle.

½ cup vanilla-flavored black tea	*⅛ teaspoon vanilla extract*
	⅛ teaspoon ground nutmeg
2 scoops vanilla ice cream	*¼ cup heavy cream, whipped*

Mix all the ingredients except the whipped cream in a blender for 15 to 20 seconds, or until smooth. Pour the mixture into a glass and top with whipped cream.

Serves 1

Vanilla-Orange Tea Shake

Serve this fluffy drink immediately.

$\frac{3}{4}$ cup vanilla-flavored
   black tea
2 scoops vanilla ice cream

2 tablespoons orange juice
$\frac{1}{4}$ cup heavy cream, whipped
Orange slice, for garnish

Mix the tea, ice cream, and orange juice in a blender for 15 to 20 seconds, or until smooth. Pour into a tall glass, top with whipped cream, and garnish with a slice of orange.

Serves 1

148

Hot Green Tea Float

The subtle taste of the green tea comes through as the ice cream melts into this drink—delicious!

3 scoops vanilla or green tea
   ice cream

$\frac{3}{4}$ cup freshly brewed green
   tea, still piping hot
Whipped cream (optional)

Place the ice cream in a tall glass and add the tea. Top with whipped cream, if desired.

Serves 1

Thai Iced Tea

Bring the taste of Thailand to your palate with this classic recipe.

2 tablespoons loose Thai tea
(page 15)
3/4 cup water

2 tablespoons sugar
Ice cubes or crushed ice
1/4 cup half-and-half

Bring the tea and the water to a boil in a saucepan and simmer over low heat for 3 to 5 minutes, depending on your taste. Strain the tea through a Thai tea strainer (page 18) into another container and stir the sugar into the tea. Pour the tea over ice in a tall glass immediately, or after the tea has cooled to room temperature. Top with the half-and-half.

149
•

Serves 1

Variations: For a really rich drink, substitute heavy cream for the half-and-half and proceed as directed above. You may also omit the cream altogether.

Cold
Drinks
Made
with
Herb
Tea

Unless otherwise specified, all of the drinks in this section are made with cold brewed tea. In order to account for the dilution factor of ice cubes, you should brew the tea using $1\frac{1}{2}$ to 2 times the amount of loose tea or tea bags as normal. Then store the tea in a sealed container in the refrigerator.

Lemon-Apple Iced Tea

This drink mixes the tangy taste of lemon with the sweet taste of the apple juice.

$\frac{3}{4}$ cup lemon-flavored herb tea
$\frac{3}{4}$ cup apple juice
Ice cubes

$\frac{1}{2}$ cup carbonated water
Lemon and apple slices, for garnish

Mix the tea and juice together and pour over ice in 2 tall glasses. Add carbonated water and garnish with slices of lemon and apple.

Serves 2

Lemon Iced Tea

This drink really packs a punch—a citrus delight!

¾ cup lemon-flavored
herb tea
Ice cubes

1 teaspoon lemon juice
1 teaspoon sugar
Lemon slice, for garnish

Pour the tea over ice in a tall glass. Stir the lemon juice and sugar into the tea and garnish with a slice of lemon.

Serves 1

Lemon-Lime Iced Tea

This purple punch will really hit the spot on a hot summer day!

2 cups lemon-flavored
herb tea
1 tablespoon lemon juice
1 tablespoon lime juice
1 cup Concord grape juice

1 cup ginger ale
Ice cubes
Sugar to taste (optional)
Lemon and lime peel,
for garnish

Mix the tea, juices, and ginger ale together in a large pitcher. Pour over ice in 4 tall glasses. Add sugar, if desired, and garnish with lemon and lime peel.

Serves 4

Almond Iced Tea

This drink is refreshing and thirst-quenching, yet it could still be a dessert in itself!

2 cups almond-flavored
  herb tea
1 cup milk
2 teaspoons sugar

Ice cubes
½ cup heavy cream, whipped
  Sliced almonds, for garnish

Mix the tea, milk, and sugar together and pour over ice in 2 tall glasses. Top with whipped cream and garnish with sliced almonds.

Serves 2

Raspberry Tea Punch

Enjoy this drink under a veranda or in a gazebo.

½ cup raspberry-flavored
  herb tea
2 tablespoons white grape juice
2 tablespoons cranberry juice
  Ice cubes

¼ cup carbonated water
  Sugar to taste
  Fresh raspberries, for
  garnish

Mix the tea and juices together and pour over ice in a tall glass. Add the carbonated water and sugar and garnish with fresh raspberries.

Serves 1

Raspberry-Apple Iced Tea

The raspberries and slices of apple float on the surface of this delightful, punchy drink—and they taste great, too!

1 1/2 cups raspberry-flavored
herb tea
1/2 cup apple juice
Ice cubes

1/2 cup carbonated water
Sugar to taste (optional)
Raspberries and apple slices,
for garnish

Mix the tea and juice together and pour over ice in 2 tall glasses. Add the carbonated water and sugar, if desired. Garnish with fresh raspberries and slices of apple.

Serves 2

Rose Iced Tea

Bring the taste of roses into your glass with this drink!

½ teaspoon dried rose petals,
   or to taste
¾ cup water
Ice cubes

¼ cup carbonated water
   Sugar to taste (optional)
Sliced fresh strawberries, for
garnish

Place the rose petals at the bottom of the teapot. Boil the water and pour the water into the teapot. Let the tea brew for 3 to 5 minutes, depending on your taste. Strain into a cup and cool to room temperature. Pour over ice in a tall glass and add the carbonated water. Stir the sugar into the tea, if desired, and garnish with sliced fresh strawberries.

Serves 1

Chamomile Iced Tea

The ethereal taste of chamomile tea is enhanced beautifully by the apple and grape juices in this drink.

½ cup chamomile tea
2 tablespoons white grape juice
2 tablespoons apple juice

Ice cubes
Grapes and apple slices, for garnish

Mix the tea and juices together. Pour over ice in a large glass and garnish with grapes and slices of apple.

Serves 1

Orange-Grenadine Iced Tea

The slice of lime adds a nice accent to this drink.

2 tablespoons grenadine
1½ cups orange-flavored herb tea
Ice cubes

½ cup carbonated water (optional)
Lime slices, for garnish

Stir the grenadine into the tea and pour this mixture over ice in 2 tall glasses. Add the carbonated water, if desired, and garnish with slices of lime.

Serves 2

Cinnamon-Cranberry Iced Tea

The cinnamon, cranberry, and pineapple tastes mix well in this tart, earthy drink.

½ cup cinnamon-flavored herb tea
¼ cup cranberry juice
½ cup pineapple juice

Ice cubes
Sugar to taste
Cinnamon stick, for garnish

Mix the tea and juices together and pour over ice in a tall glass. Add sugar and garnish with a cinnamon stick.

Serves 1

Cranberry-Cherry Iced Tea

The cranberry and cherry tastes blend beautifully to create a punchlike drink.

½ cup cranberry-flavored herb tea
Ice cubes

¼ cup cherry soda
Sugar to taste (optional)
Fresh cherry, for garnish

Pour the tea over ice in a tall glass. Add the cherry soda and sugar, if desired, and garnish with a fresh cherry.

Serves 1

Hibiscus-Grape Iced Tea

Hibiscus and grape are marvelous tastes, both separately and in conjunction.

1 cup white grape juice
1 cup hibiscus tea
Ice cubes

½ cup carbonated water
Orange slices, for garnish

Stir the juice into the tea and pour over ice in 2 large glasses. Add carbonated water and garnish with slices of orange.

Serves 2

Hot Mint Tea Float

Enjoy the ice cream as it melts into this drink!

3 scoops mint chocolate chip
   ice cream
¾ cup freshly brewed mint-
   flavored herb tea, still
   piping hot

¼ cup heavy cream, whipped
Sweetened chocolate powder

Place the ice cream in a tall glass and add the tea. Top with whipped cream and sprinkle with chocolate powder.

Serves 1

Mint Tea Float

Chocolate, mint, and whipped cream—all in one drink! What could be better?

¾ cup mint-flavored herb tea
2 tablespoons chocolate syrup
2 scoops vanilla ice cream

¼ cup heavy cream, whipped
Sweetened chocolate powder

Pour the tea into a tall glass. Stir the chocolate syrup into the tea, add the ice cream, and top with the whipped cream and chocolate powder.

Serves 1

Variation: Substitute 2 scoops of chocolate ice cream for the vanilla ice cream and chocolate syrup. Proceed as directed above.

Orange Tea Crush

The sherbet mixes with the tea to form a slushy orange- or lemon-flavored drink.

¾ cup orange-flavored herb tea   *½ cup crushed ice*
½ cup orange sherbet

Mix all the ingredients together in a blender for 15 to 20 seconds, or until smooth. Pour into a tall glass.

Serves 1

Variation: For a Lemon Tea Crush, substitute lemon-flavored herb tea and lemon sherbet for the orange-flavored herb tea and orange sherbet. Proceed as directed above.

Almond-Vanilla Tea Shake

Almond and vanilla make a great combination of tastes—a real treat!

½ cup almond-flavored
herb tea
2 scoops vanilla ice cream

Whipped cream (optional)
Sliced almonds, for garnish
(optional)

Mix the tea and ice cream together in a blender for 15 to 20 seconds, or until smooth. Pour the mixture into a tall glass. Top with whipped cream and garnish with sliced almonds, if desired.

Serves 1

162

Peach-Yogurt Tea Shake

This drink can also be made using peach-, strawberry-, or raspberry-flavored black tea. Enjoy!

*½ cup peach-flavored
 herb tea
½ cup peach yogurt*

*1 tablespoon honey
Peach slices, for garnish
Ice cubes (optional)*

Mix the tea, yogurt, and honey together in a blender for 15 to 20 seconds, or until smooth. Garnish with fresh slices of peach. (You can also pour this drink over ice, if desired.)

Serves 1

Variations: For a Strawberry-Yogurt Tea Shake, substitute strawberry-flavored herb tea and strawberry yogurt for the peach-flavored herb tea and peach yogurt. Proceed as directed above and garnish with sliced fresh strawberries.

For a Raspberry-Yogurt Tea Shake, use raspberry-flavored herb tea and raspberry yogurt. Proceed as directed above and garnish with fresh raspberries.

Gourmet *Tea* Drinks *with* Liquor

In addition to the liquors mentioned in this chapter, feel free to add your own combination of liquors to whichever teas you prefer, depending on your taste. The recipes in this chapter are for hot and cold drinks made with black tea and herb tea. Salut!

Hot *Drinks* **Made** *with* **Black** *Tea*

Rum-Cider Tea

The rum adds a special accent to this mulled cider tea— great for sitting in front of a fire on a cold winter day.

½ *cup apple cider*	½ *cup black tea*
1 *cinnamon stick*	2 *tablespoons rum*
2 *whole cloves*	*Orange and lemon peel, for*
⅛ *teaspoon ground allspice*	*garnish*

Combine the cider, cinnamon stick, cloves, and allspice in a saucepan and simmer over low heat for 1 to 2 minutes, stirring occasionally. Pour the tea into the saucepan and stir all the ingredients together. Strain the mixture into a cup, add the rum, and garnish with a small slice of orange and lemon peel.

Serves 1

Rum-Brandy Tea

A spirited tea, this drink needs no embellishments. It is fine just as it is.

¾ cup black tea
1 tablespoon rum

1 tablespoon brandy

Pour the tea into a cup. Stir the rum and the brandy into the tea.

Serves 1

Anisette Tea

The licorice taste of the anisette mixes well with the mint in this drink.

¾ cup black tea
2 tablespoons anisette liqueur
¼ cup heavy cream, whipped

Fresh mint sprig, for garnish

Pour the tea into a cup. Stir the anisette into the tea, top with whipped cream, and garnish with a fresh mint sprig.

Serves 1

Orange-Spice Tea Delight

The orange-and-spice tea combines beautifully with the red wine, cinnamon, and brown sugar to produce a hot mulled punch.

¼ cup red wine
1 cinnamon stick

¾ cup orange-and-spice–
flavored black tea
1 tablespoon brown sugar

Place the wine and the cinnamon stick in a saucepan and simmer over low heat for 1 to 2 minutes, stirring occasionally. Pour the tea into the saucepan and stir in the brown sugar. Pour into a mug.

Serves 1

Hot *Drinks* Made *with* Herb *Tea*

Chamomile-Brandy Tea

Whether you use the brandy or the crème de menthe, your chamomile tea will never be the same.

¾ cup chamomile tea
1 tablespoon brandy
Sugar to taste (optional)

Lemon peel, for garnish
(optional)

Pour the tea into a cup. Stir the brandy into the tea. Add sugar and garnish with a small strip of lemon peel, if desired.

Serves 1

Variation: For a Chamomile-Crème de Menthe Tea, substitute 1 tablespoon crème de menthe for the brandy and omit the sugar and lemon peel. Proceed as directed above.

Grand Marnier Tea

Enjoy a special after-dinner treat as you sip the Grand Marnier through the whipped cream—incredible!

*¾ cup orange-flavored herb tea
2 tablespoons Grand Marnier
  liqueur*

*¼ cup heavy cream, whipped
Grated orange peel, for
  garnish*

Pour the tea into a cup. Stir the Grand Marnier into the tea, top with whipped cream, and sprinkle with grated orange peel.

Serves 1

Amaretto Tea

The great taste of amaretto bursts into your mouth with this drink.

*6 tablespoons amaretto
  liqueur
1½ cups almond-flavored
  herb tea*

*½ cup heavy cream, whipped
Ground almonds, for
  garnish*

Stir the amaretto into the tea in 2 cups. Top with whipped cream and sprinkle with ground almonds.

Serves 2

Galliano Tea

Lemon and Galliano are made for each other—wow!

¾ cup lemon-flavored herb tea
2 tablespoons Galliano
liqueur

Lemon peel, for garnish

Pour the tea into a cup. Stir the Galliano into the tea and garnish with a small strip of lemon peel.

Serves 1

Mint-Cocoa Tea

Two of our most popular liqueurs are blended together in this drink—great for warming you up on a cold winter evening.

¾ cup mint-flavored herb tea
1½ tablespoons crème de cacao
1½ tablespoons crème de menthe
¼ cup heavy cream, whipped

Sweetened chocolate powder
Fresh mint sprig, for
garnish

Pour the tea into a cup. Stir the crème de cacao and crème de menthe into the tea. Top with whipped cream and chocolate powder and garnish with a fresh mint sprig.

Serves 1

Cold *Drinks* **Made** *with* **Black** *Tea*

Lemon Tea Punch

This drink is great for the beach, a picnic at the park, or a Fourth of July barbecue.

½ cup lemon-flavored
  black tea
2 tablespoons lemon juice
2 tablespoons orange juice
¼ cup ginger ale
¼ cup champagne

Ice cubes
Sugar to taste
Orange, lemon, or
strawberry slices, for
garnish

Mix the tea, juices, ginger ale, and champagne together and pour over ice in a tall glass. Add sugar and garnish with slices of orange, lemon, or strawberry.

Serves 1

Cocoa-Mint Tea Shake

Drinking crème de cacao and crème de menthe through whipped cream is about as close to perfection as you can get.

½ cup black tea
1 scoop vanilla or chocolate ice cream
1 tablespoon crème de cacao

1 tablespoon crème de menthe
¼ cup heavy cream, whipped
Fresh mint sprig, for garnish

Mix the tea, ice cream, crème de cacao, and crème de menthe in a blender for 15 to 20 seconds, or until smooth. Top with whipped cream and garnish with a fresh mint sprig.

Serves 1

Mint Julep Tea

Feel free to use mint-flavored herb tea as well with this drink.

¾ cup mint-flavored black tea
Crushed ice
2 tablespoons bourbon

Sugar to taste
Fresh mint sprig, for garnish

Pour the tea over ice in a tall glass. Stir in the bourbon and the sugar. Garnish with a fresh mint sprig.

Serves 1

Cold *Drinks* **Made** *with* *Herb* **Tea**

Red Wine–Tea Punch

This tangy, winy punch is perfect for a party. Enjoy!

1 cup orange-flavored herb tea
1 cup red wine
½ cup orange juice
½ cup cranberry juice
½ cup apple juice
½ cup carbonated water
Ice cubes
Sugar to taste (optional)
Lemon slices, for garnish

Mix the tea, wine, juices, and carbonated water together in a pitcher and pour over ice in 4 tall glasses. Add sugar, if desired, and garnish with slices of lemon.

Serves 4

Iced Crème de Menthe Tea

Cool, minty, and refreshing, this drink is a real winner!

1½ cups mint-flavored
    herb tea
Ice cubes
¼ cup crème de menthe

½ cup heavy cream, whipped
Fresh mint sprigs,
    for garnish

Pour the tea over ice in 2 tall glasses. Stir the crème de menthe into the tea, top with whipped cream, and garnish with a fresh mint sprig.

Serves 1

MAKING
YOUR OWN
GOURMET
CHOCOLATE
DRINKS

To my mother,
Patience Fish Tekulsky,
who first introduced me
to the joys of chocolate!

Acknowledgments

I would like to thank the great team of designer Nancy Kenmore, illustrator Clair Moritz-Magnesio, and production editor Kim Hertlein, for making my cookbooks look so great. Thanks as well to Gail Shanks, for setting up author appearances. Thanks, as always, to Michelle Sidrane and Ann Patty, for their continued support. And thanks as always to my literary agent, Jane Jordan Browne, and to my editor, Brandt Aymar. Special thanks to all of the wonderful people I have met at my book signings and who purchase my books. You are the greatest!

Contents

Introduction

Ever since the Aztec emperor Montezuma introduced the Spanish explorer Hernán Cortés to the wonders of a chocolate beverage called xocolatl (meaning "bitter water") in 1519, the proliferation of chocolate, first as a beverage, then as a food, has continued throughout the world. • After the Spanish sweetened the drink with sugar, it became a favorite at court, appealing greatly to the nobles of the time. • Eventually, the use of this beverage spread throughout Europe, and in the mid-seventeenth century, a conglomeration of chocolate houses in London played a primary role in the business and social activities of the day. • It was not until the middle of the next century that chocolate arrived in Colonial America, although it was still consumed as a beverage even at this late date. • And while the invention of the milk chocolate bar did not occur until 1876, the popularity of chocolate as a *beverage—both hot and cold—continues to this day.* • *With this book, you will be able to make a great combination of drinks using the fabulous cocoa bean, just as Montezuma did.*

Whether you choose to mix your chocolate with fruit such as raspberries, blueberries, or cherries; nuts such as hazelnuts, almonds, or peanuts; candies made from maple sugar, mint, or licorice; or liqueurs such as Grand Marnier,

amaretto, or Kahlúa, you will be sure to experience a wide assortment of delectable tastes—yet all with one thing in common: They are all made with chocolate! • *We will include hot drinks for cold winter days, as well as cold drinks for the blazing days of summer—and many drinks that you can enjoy on all the days in between.* • *So settle back and get your taste buds ready.* • *After all, chocolate is not called "Food of the Gods" for nothing.* • *Enjoy!*

The Various
Types of Chocolate
You Can Use

All chocolate is derived from the cocoa bean, which is the seed of the cocoa tree, *Theobroma cacao* (Theobroma means food of the gods).

The cocoa tree grows in tropical climates, between twenty degrees north and twenty degrees south of the equator.

Although the cocoa tree is native to Mexico and Central and South America, more than half of the world's cocoa beans today are produced in the western African countries of the Ivory Coast, Ghana, Nigeria, and Cameroon. The remaining cocoa beans are largely produced in Brazil, Indonesia, and Malaysia, and to a lesser extent in other countries such as Ecuador, the Dominican Republic, Mexico, Colombia, Papua New Guinea, and Venezuela.

The cocoa tree produces pods throughout the year, in which seeds (or beans) are contained. After the pods are cut from the tree, they are split open and the beans are removed.

After fermenting for a few days, the beans are dried in the sun for a few more days, and are then packed for shipment to chocolate factories around the world.

When the cocoa beans arrive at the chocolate factory, they are roasted, after which the shells are removed to reveal the cocoa nibs—the "meat" of the bean.

The cocoa nibs are then ground to create a pasty liquid known as chocolate liquor–which consists of cocoa solids as well as cocoa butter. This is unsweetened baking chocolate, which is poured into molds and cooled before being packaged as bars.

In order to create semisweet (or bittersweet) baking chocolate, sugar (and often additional cocoa butter) is added to the chocolate liquor; and in order to create milk chocolate, sugar, additional cocoa butter, and milk are added to the chocolate liquor. Semisweet chocolate and milk chocolate are also poured into molds and cooled before being packaged as bars.

In order to create unsweetened cocoa powder, the chocolate liquor is sent through a hydraulic press that extracts most of the cocoa butter and leaves a "press cake" consisting primarily of the cocoa solids. This press cake is then finely ground and sifted, thus creating the unsweetened cocoa powder.

Dutch-processed cocoa powder is produced by treating the chocolate liquor with an alkali. This gives the resulting cocoa powder a milder, less acidic taste, as well as a darker brown color than ordinary unsweetened cocoa powder.

White chocolate is not really chocolate at all, since it is composed only of cocoa butter, sugar, milk solids, and flavorings such as vanilla–and has no cocoa solids in it.

Chocolate syrup consists of unsweetened cocoa powder, sugar, and water.

Sweetened chocolate powder consists of unsweetened cocoa powder and sugar.

Storing Your Chocolate

No matter which type of chocolate you use, it is important to store it in the proper manner in order to make sure that it lasts as long as possible and stays as fresh as possible before you use it.

In general, unsweetened, semisweet, white, and milk chocolate should be stored in a cool, dry place (about 60° F. to 70° F.). Chocolate should not be stored in the refrigerator, as the cold temperature caused by refrigeration can cause a gray or white film (or "bloom") to appear on the surface of the chocolate as the cocoa butter rises to the surface. This bloom can occur if the chocolate is exposed to too much heat as well; however, the bloom will disappear when you melt the chocolate, and it has no effect on the taste of the chocolate.

If chocolate is exposed to too much moisture (such as from refrigeration), the moisture can cause the sugar crystals in the chocolate to rise to the surface of the chocolate, thus causing a gray or white "sugar bloom." This bloom also disappears when the chocolate is melted, and has no effect on the taste of the chocolate.

Unsweetened cocoa powder and sweetened chocolate powder should be stored in an airtight container in a cool, dry place (about 60° F. to 70° F.). They should not be stored in the refrigerator, as the moisture from refrigeration can cause the powder to become lumpy.

Chocolate syrup should be stored in the refrigerator after it is opened.

When stored properly, unsweetened baking chocolate should remain fresh for about 2 years; semisweet baking chocolate for about 1½ years; white and milk chocolate for about 1 year; unsweetened cocoa powder and sweetened chocolate powder for about 2 years; and chocolate syrup for about 1 year.

Using Your Chocolate

Because different types of chocolate have varying amounts of sugar and cocoa butter in them, they can be used in conjunction with certain ingredients in order to achieve a desired result.

For instance, drinks that are made with unsweetened baking chocolate or unsweetened cocoa powder can be sweetened by adding maple syrup, eggnog, or liqueurs such as crème de cacao.

Meanwhile, drinks that are made with semisweet chocolate or chocolate syrup can incorporate ingredients such as cinnamon, espresso, and malted milk powder without having to add any extra sugar.

And unsweetened cocoa powder, which is low-fat, can be used with yogurt and nonfat milk to create a delicious low-cal drink.

How you decide to use your chocolate is largely a matter of personal preference, so feel free to use your imagination to create the chocolate drinks that you like best.

Making Chocolate
Whipped Cream

You may wish to top some of the drinks in this book with chocolate-flavored whipped cream.

Here is how you make it: Place ¼ cup heavy cream in a bowl and add 1 teaspoon chocolate syrup (or 1 teaspoon unsweetened cocoa powder and ½ teaspoon regular granulated sugar) to the heavy cream. Whip up the cream along with the chocolate (or cocoa and sugar), and use this chocolate-flavored whipped cream to top off some of your favorite gourmet chocolate drinks.

A Note on Ingredients

1. With chocolate baking bars, 1 ounce is a measurement of weight, not volume.

2. I use chocolate syrup, but an equal amount of sweetened chocolate powder can be used as well.

3. I use white chocolate chips, but you can also use the equivalent amount of a white chocolate baking bar or white chocolate candy, depending on your taste.

4. When using unsweetened cocoa powder to make hot cocoa, it is best to first make a paste with the cocoa powder and a small amount of milk or whatever liquid you are using; then stir this paste into the rest of the liquid over low heat. This will allow the cocoa powder to dissolve into the liquid in the smoothest fashion possible, without causing lumps of cocoa powder to occur in the liquid.

5. I use regular granulated sugar.

6. Unless otherwise specified, I use whole milk, but low-fat or even nonfat milk can also be used, depending on your taste.

7. I use low-fat yogurt, but nonfat yogurt can also be used.

8. It is always best to use fresh whipped cream—generally about ¼ cup per drink.

9. Feel free to use packaged or fresh coconut milk (if available); and feel free to substitute fresh chopped coconut for sweetened shredded coconut (as a garnish).

10. I use sliced marshmallows, but miniature marshmallows can also be used.

11. Unless otherwise specified, all nuts are raw and shelled.

12. If you wish to make more (or fewer) servings of these drinks, simply multiply (or divide) the amount of each ingredient to provide for the number of servings that you wish to make.

Hot
Gourmet
Chocolate
Drinks

Hot Chocolate Royale

The half-and-half makes this drink much richer than a standard hot chocolate. (For a standard hot chocolate, simply use regular milk instead of the half-and-half.)

½ ounce semisweet baking
    chocolate
1 cup half-and-half

¼ cup heavy cream,
    whipped
Sweetened chocolate
    powder

Stir the chocolate into the half-and-half in a saucepan over low heat for 3 to 4 minutes, or until hot (do not boil). Pour into a mug and top with the whipped cream and chocolate powder.

Serves 1

Hot Cocoa

In all of its variations, this drink is a traditional favorite that is sure to warm you up on a cold winter day.

2 teaspoons unsweetened
  cocoa powder
2 teaspoons sugar
2 cups milk
  Whipped cream
  (optional)

Sweetened chocolate
powder or unsweetened
cocoa powder (optional)

Stir the cocoa powder and the sugar into 4 teaspoons of the milk in a saucepan, until a smooth paste is formed. Pour the rest of the milk into the saucepan and stir the mixture constantly over low heat for 5 to 6 minutes, or until it is hot (do not boil). Pour into 2 mugs and top with whipped cream and sprinkle with chocolate powder or cocoa powder, if desired.

Serves 2

Variations: For a Vanilla Hot Cocoa, stir ⅛ teaspoon vanilla extract into each drink before topping with whipped cream and sprinkling with chocolate powder or cocoa powder, if desired.

For a Mint Hot Cocoa, stir ⅛ teaspoon mint extract into each drink before topping with whipped cream and sprinkling with chocolate powder or cocoa powder, if desired.

For an Orange Hot Cocoa, stir ⅛ teaspoon orange extract into each drink before topping with whipped cream and sprinkling with chocolate powder or cocoa powder, if desired.

Dark-White Hot Chocolate

The white chocolate chips add their own distinctive taste to the traditional taste of the semisweet chocolate.

$\frac{1}{2}$ ounce semisweet baking chocolate

1 tablespoon white chocolate chips

2 cups milk

$\frac{1}{2}$ cup heavy cream, whipped

Sweetened chocolate powder or additional white chocolate chips, for garnish

Stir the semisweet chocolate and 1 tablespoon white chocolate chips into the milk in a saucepan over low heat for 5 to 6 minutes, or until hot (do not boil). Pour into 2 mugs, top with the whipped cream, and garnish with chocolate powder or white chocolate chips.

Serves 2

Butterscotch Hot Chocolate

The taste of this drink goes back and forth between chocolate and butterscotch–what could be better?

1 tablespoon chocolate syrup	Whipped cream (optional)
1 tablespoon butterscotch topping	Sweetened chocolate powder or ground
1 cup milk	nutmeg, for garnish (optional)

Stir the chocolate syrup and the butterscotch topping into the milk in a saucepan over low heat for 3 to 4 minutes, or until hot (do not boil). Pour the mixture into a mug and top with whipped cream and chocolate powder or nutmeg, if desired.

Serves 1

Honey Hot Chocolate

The honey adds a special taste to the hot chocolate.

$\frac{1}{2}$ ounce unsweetened
   baking chocolate
1 tablespoon honey
$\frac{1}{8}$ teaspoon ground
   cinnamon

1 cup milk
$\frac{1}{4}$ cup heavy cream,
   whipped

Stir the chocolate, honey, and cinnamon into the milk in a saucepan over low heat for 3 to 4 minutes, or until hot (do not boil). Pour into a mug and top with whipped cream.

Serves 1

Maple Hot Chocolate

This drink will make you think of autumn in New England.

$\frac{1}{2}$ ounce unsweetened
   baking chocolate
2 tablespoons maple syrup
1 cup milk

$\frac{1}{4}$ cup heavy cream,
   whipped
Maple sugar candy, for
   garnish (optional)

Stir the chocolate and the maple syrup into the milk in a saucepan over low heat for 3 to 4 minutes, or until hot (do not boil). Pour into a mug, top with whipped cream, and garnish with small pieces of maple sugar candy, if desired.

Serves 1

Mint Hot Chocolate

You may wish to substitute Chocolate Whipped Cream (page 20) for the regular whipped cream in this drink, in which case the chocolate powder would be optional. Please feel free to substitute Chocolate Whipped Cream for the regular whipped cream in the variation as well. It is up to you.

1 tablespoon chocolate
   syrup
1 cup milk
1/8 teaspoon mint extract
1/4 cup heavy cream,
   whipped

Sweetened chocolate
powder
Fresh mint sprig, for
garnish

Stir the chocolate syrup into the milk in a saucepan over low heat for 3 to 4 minutes, or until hot (do not boil). Pour this mixture into a mug and stir in the mint extract. Top with whipped cream and chocolate powder and garnish with a fresh mint sprig.

Serves 1

Variation: For an Orange Hot Chocolate, substitute 1/8 teaspoon orange extract for the mint extract and proceed as directed above. Top with whipped cream and sprinkle with grated orange peel.

Cinnamon Hot Chocolate

The great taste of cinnamon adds a nice accent to the hot chocolate.

1 tablespoon chocolate
syrup
⅛ teaspoon ground
cinnamon
1 cup milk
¼ cup heavy cream,
whipped

Additional ground
cinnamon
Cinnamon stick, for
garnish (optional)

Stir the chocolate syrup and ⅛ teaspoon cinnamon into the milk in a saucepan over low heat for 3 to 4 minutes, or until hot (do not boil). Pour into a mug, top with whipped cream, sprinkle with cinnamon, and garnish with a cinnamon stick, if desired.

Serves 1

Spiced Hot Chocolate

Spices and chocolate taste great together–whether you use the vanilla or the almond extract.

2 tablespoons chocolate
    syrup
¼ teaspoon ground
    cinnamon
⅛ teaspoon ground allspice
⅛ teaspoon ground nutmeg

¼ teaspoon vanilla extract
2 cups milk
½ cup heavy cream,
    whipped
Sweetened chocolate
    powder

Stir the chocolate syrup, spices, and vanilla extract into the milk in a saucepan over low heat for 5 to 6 minutes, or until hot (do not boil). Pour into 2 mugs, top with whipped cream, and sprinkle with chocolate powder.

Serves 2

Variation: Substitute ¼ teaspoon almond extract for the vanilla extract. Proceed as directed above.

Espresso Hot Chocolate

Whether you use the espresso or the coffee in this drink, it is sure to satisfy!

1 tablespoon chocolate
    syrup
1½ ounces freshly brewed
    espresso, still piping hot
1 cup milk

¼ cup heavy cream,
    whipped
Sweetened chocolate
    powder or ground
    cinnamon

Stir the chocolate syrup and the espresso into the milk in a saucepan over low heat for 3 to 4 minutes, or until hot (do not boil). Pour into a mug, top with whipped cream, and sprinkle with chocolate powder or cinnamon.

Serves 1

Variation: For a Coffee Hot Chocolate, substitute ¼ cup freshly brewed coffee for the espresso and use ¾ cup milk. Proceed as directed above.

Hot Cocoa-Espresso Eggnog

This drink is like a chocolate eggnog latte–great for the holidays!

1 teaspoon unsweetened cocoa powder	1½ ounces freshly brewed espresso, still piping hot
¾ cup eggnog	¼ cup heavy cream, whipped
¼ cup milk	Ground nutmeg

Stir the cocoa powder into 2 teaspoons of the eggnog in a saucepan, until a smooth paste is formed. Pour the rest of the eggnog along with the milk and the espresso into the saucepan and stir the mixture constantly over low heat for 3 to 4 minutes, or until hot (do not boil). Pour into a mug and top with whipped cream and nutmeg.

Serves 1

Variation: For a richer drink, substitute ¼ cup half-and-half for the milk. Proceed as directed above.

Tea Hot Chocolate

The subtle taste of the tea comes through in this delicious drink.

1 tablespoon chocolate
syrup
²⁄₃ cup milk
⅓ cup freshly brewed
English Breakfast or
another black tea, still
piping hot

⅛ teaspoon vanilla extract
(optional)
¼ cup heavy cream,
whipped
Sweetened chocolate
powder

Stir the chocolate syrup into the milk in a saucepan over low heat for 3 to 4 minutes, or until hot (do not boil). Add the tea and stir so that all of the ingredients are mixed together. Pour this mixture into a mug, add the vanilla extract, if desired, and top with whipped cream and chocolate powder.

Serves 1

Coconut Hot Chocolate

The great taste of coconut and chocolate mix beautifully in this drink.

2 cups milk
½ cup sweetened shredded coconut

1 ounce unsweetened baking chocolate

Preheat the oven to 350° F. Place 1 cup of the milk and the coconut in a saucepan and stir occasionally over low heat for 3 to 4 minutes, or until hot (do not boil). Strain the milk into a container and place the coconut on a baking sheet. Bake the coconut in the oven until it turns brown, about 8 to 10 minutes. Meanwhile, stir the coconut-flavored milk and the chocolate into the remaining milk in a saucepan over low heat for 3 to 4 minutes, or until hot (do not boil). Pour this mixture into 2 mugs and top with the browned coconut.

Serves 2

Malted Hot Chocolate

Add the taste of malted milk to your hot chocolate with this drink.

½ ounce semisweet baking
   chocolate
1 tablespoon malted milk
   powder
1 cup milk

Whipped cream
(optional)
Malted milk powder, for
garnish (optional)

Stir the chocolate and 1 tablespoon malted milk powder into the milk in a saucepan over low heat for 3 to 4 minutes, or until hot (do not boil). Pour into a mug and top with the whipped cream and sprinkle with malted milk powder, if desired.

Serves 1

Chocolate Mint Candy
Hot Chocolate

Enjoy eating the candy as you drink this drink!

*1 piece of chocolate mint
  candy*
*½ ounce semisweet baking
  chocolate*

1 cup milk
*¼ cup heavy cream,
  whipped*

Place the candy at the bottom of a mug. Stir the chocolate
into the milk in a saucepan over low heat for 3 to 4 minutes,
or until hot (do not boil). Pour over the candy in the mug
and top with whipped cream.

Serves 1

Variation: For an English Toffee Hot Chocolate, substitute 1 piece of English toffee candy for the chocolate mint
candy. Proceed as directed above.

Raisin Hot Chocolate

The great taste of the raisins mixes well with the taste of the chocolate–whether white or dark. (Feel free to use 1 tablespoon fresh sliced apricot–peeled or unpeeled–instead of the raisins in this drink.)

1 tablespoon raisins
½ ounce semisweet baking
   chocolate

1 cup milk
¼ cup heavy cream,
   whipped

Place the raisins at the bottom of a mug. Stir the chocolate into the milk in a saucepan over low heat for 3 to 4 minutes, or until hot (do not boil). Pour over the raisins in the mug and top with whipped cream.

Serves 1

Variation: For a Raisin–White Hot Chocolate, substitute 1 tablespoon white chocolate chips for the semisweet chocolate and proceed as directed above.

Pecan Hot Chocolate

The pecans and macadamia nuts float in this drink, so you can enjoy spooning them off the surface of the hot chocolate!

1 tablespoon pecans	¼ cup heavy cream,
½ ounce semisweet baking	whipped
chocolate	Ground pecans, for
1 cup milk	garnish

Place 1 tablespoon pecans at the bottom of a mug. Stir the chocolate into the milk in a saucepan over low heat for 3 to 4 minutes, or until hot (do not boil). Pour over the pecans in the mug and top with whipped cream and ground pecans.

Serves 1

Variation: For a Macadamia Nut Hot Chocolate, substitute 1 tablespoon macadamia nuts for the pecans and proceed as directed above. Garnish with ground macadamia nuts.

Ice Cream Hot Cocoa

The ice cream melts into the hot cocoa and provides a sweetener as well.

1 teaspoon unsweetened
    cocoa powder
1 cup milk

1 scoop chocolate, vanilla,
    or coffee ice cream

Stir the cocoa powder into 2 teaspoons of the milk in a saucepan, until a smooth paste is formed. Pour the rest of the milk into the saucepan and stir the mixture constantly over low heat for 3 to 4 minutes, or until it is hot (do not boil). Pour into a mug and add the ice cream.

Serves 1

Cold
Gourmet
Chocolate
Drinks

Coffee Chocolate Milk

This is a great drink for the summer!

1 cup milk

1 tablespoon chocolate
   syrup

1 cup brewed coffee,
   chilled

Ice cubes

Ground cinnamon
   (optional)

Mix the milk, chocolate syrup, and coffee together and pour over ice in 2 tall glasses. Sprinkle with cinnamon, if desired.

Serves 2

Chocolate Soda Float

The ice cream melts into the soda and adds its own distinct flavor to this drink–delicious!

¾ cup chocolate soda,
   chilled

1 scoop chocolate, vanilla,
   or coffee ice cream

Whipped cream
   (optional)

Sweetened chocolate
   powder (optional)

Pour the chocolate soda into a tall glass. Add the ice cream and top with whipped cream and chocolate powder, if desired.

Serves 1

Chocolate Milk Float

This drink turns a glass of chocolate milk into a special treat.

1 teaspoon chocolate
  syrup
1 cup milk
1 scoop chocolate ice
  cream

¼ cup heavy cream,
  whipped
Sweetened chocolate
  powder

Stir the chocolate syrup into the milk in a tall glass. Add the ice cream and top with whipped cream and chocolate powder.

Serves 1

Variation: For a Vanilla–Chocolate Milk Float, substitute 1 scoop vanilla ice cream for the chocolate ice cream and use 1 tablespoon chocolate syrup instead of 1 teaspoon chocolate syrup. Proceed as directed above.

Chocolate Egg Cream

If you stir the chocolate syrup up from the bottom of the glass slowly and carefully (being sure to stop at just the right time!), you can create three layers of color in this drink–dark brown at the bottom, light brown in the middle, and white at the top.

¼ cup milk
¾ cup carbonated water, chilled

2 tablespoons chocolate syrup

Pour the milk into a tall glass. Add the carbonated water and chocolate syrup and stir briskly until a head of foam is created.

Serves 1

Variations: For a richer drink, substitute ¼ cup half-and-half or heavy cream for the milk and proceed as directed above.

For a Chocolate Phosphate, omit the milk and use 1 cup carbonated water instead of ¾ cup carbonated water. Proceed as directed above.

Chocolate-Strawberry
Ice Cream Soda

Treat yourself to bites of the strawberry ice cream as you drink this drink.

4 tablespoons chocolate
syrup

2 cups milk

1 cup carbonated water

2 scoops strawberry ice
cream

Fresh strawberries, for
garnish

Stir 2 tablespoons of the chocolate syrup into 1 cup of the milk in each of 2 tall glasses. Add ½ cup carbonated water and 1 scoop ice cream to each glass and garnish with fresh strawberries.

Serves 2

Ginger-Chocolate Float

Chocolate ice cream can be mixed with four different sodas—each with a different effect.

<table>
<tr><td>¾ cup ginger ale, chilled</td><td>Whipped cream (optional)</td></tr>
<tr><td>1 scoop chocolate ice cream</td><td>Sweetened chocolate powder (optional)</td></tr>
</table>

Pour the ginger ale into a tall glass. Add the ice cream and top with whipped cream and chocolate powder, if desired.

Serves 1

Variations: For a Root Beer–Chocolate Float, substitute ¾ cup chilled root beer for the ginger ale and proceed as directed above.

For a Cream Soda–Chocolate Float, substitute ¾ cup chilled cream soda for the ginger ale and proceed as directed above.

For a Cherry-Chocolate Float, substitute ¾ cup chilled cherry soda for the ginger ale and proceed as directed above.

Chocolate-Marshmallow Blend

Chocolate and marshmallows—what a combination! There's nothing like it!

1 cup milk
1 tablespoon chocolate
   syrup
2 tablespoons sliced
   marshmallows
   Ice cubes
¼ cup heavy cream,
   whipped

Sweetened chocolate
powder
Additional sliced
marshmallows, for
garnish

Mix the milk, chocolate syrup, and 2 tablespoons marshmallows in a blender for 10 to 15 seconds, or until smooth. Pour over ice in a tall glass, top with whipped cream and chocolate powder, and garnish with marshmallows.

Serves 1

Chocolate-Eggnog Blend

This drink will remind you of the winter holidays on a warm summer evening.

½ cup eggnog	Ice cubes
½ cup milk	Ground nutmeg
1 teaspoon unsweetened cocoa powder	

Mix the eggnog, milk, and cocoa powder in a blender for 15 to 20 seconds, or until smooth. Pour over ice in a tall glass and sprinkle with nutmeg.

Serves 1

Variation: For a Banana-Chocolate-Eggnog Blend, add 1 peeled and sliced banana to the eggnog, milk, and cocoa powder. Proceed as directed above.

Chocolate-Banana Blend

Serve this drink immediately, before it has time to settle.

1 cup milk

1 banana, peeled and
  sliced

1 teaspoon unsweetened
  cocoa powder

¼ cup heavy cream,
  whipped

Additional banana
  slices, for garnish

Mix the milk, banana, and cocoa powder in a blender for 15 to 20 seconds, or until smooth. Pour into a tall glass, top with whipped cream, and garnish with slices of banana.

Serves 1

Chocolate-Mango Blend

Please feel free to use other fruit with this drink, such as strawberries, raspberries, blueberries, or peach slices.

$\frac{1}{2}$ cup mango, sliced
$\frac{1}{2}$ cup milk

1 tablespoon chocolate syrup

Mix all the ingredients in a blender for 15 to 20 seconds, or until smooth.

Serves 1

Variation: For a Chocolate-Pineapple Blend, substitute $\frac{1}{2}$ cup pineapple, peeled and sliced, for the mango.

Chocolate-Orange Yogurt Blend

Drink this one right away, while it is still frothy.

$\frac{1}{4}$ cup plain yogurt, low-fat
$\frac{1}{4}$ cup milk, nonfat
$\frac{1}{2}$ cup orange juice

1 teaspoon chocolate syrup

Mix all the ingredients in a blender for 10 to 15 seconds, or until smooth.

Serves 1

Chocolate-Raspberry
Yogurt Blend

Use this low-fat elixir as a pick-me-up between meals—or anytime else.

½ cup raspberry yogurt,
   low-fat
½ cup milk, nonfat

1 tablespoon unsweetened
   cocoa powder

Mix all the ingredients in a blender for 10 to 15 seconds, or until smooth.

Serves 1

Variations: For a Chocolate—Peach Yogurt Blend, substitute ½ cup peach yogurt for the raspberry yogurt. Proceed as directed above.

For a Chocolate—Strawberry Yogurt Blend, substitute ½ cup strawberry yogurt for the raspberry yogurt. Proceed as directed above.

For a Chocolate—Blueberry Yogurt Blend, substitute ½ cup blueberry yogurt for the raspberry yogurt. Proceed as directed above.

Chocolate-Espresso
Yogurt Blend

This low-fat drink tastes great—a chocolate-espresso delight!

½ cup plain yogurt, low-fat
½ cup milk, nonfat
1½ ounces brewed espresso,
  chilled

2 tablespoons chocolate
  syrup
1 teaspoon sugar

Mix all the ingredients in a blender for 10 to 15 seconds, or until smooth.

Serves 1

Chocolate-Coffee Shake

Two of our favorite flavors blend together perfectly in this drink.

1 scoop chocolate ice
  cream
1 scoop coffee ice cream
1 cup milk

Whipped cream
(optional)
Sweetened chocolate
powder (optional)

Mix the ice creams and the milk in a blender for 15 to 20 seconds, or until smooth. Pour into a tall glass and top with whipped cream and chocolate powder, if desired.

Serves 1

Chocolate-Raspberry Shake

Whether you use raspberries, strawberries, or kiwifruit to flavor this drink, it is sure to pack a fruity "punch." For a low-cal version, substitute chocolate frozen yogurt for the chocolate ice cream.

1 scoop chocolate ice cream	1/4 cup heavy cream, whipped
1/4 cup fresh raspberries	Additional raspberries, for garnish
1/2 cup milk	

Mix the ice cream, 1/4 cup raspberries, and milk in a blender for 15 to 20 seconds, or until smooth. Pour into a tall glass, top with whipped cream, and garnish with fresh raspberries.

Serves 1

Variations: For a Chocolate-Strawberry Shake, substitute 1/4 cup fresh strawberries for the raspberries and proceed as directed above. Garnish with fresh strawberries.

For a Chocolate-Kiwi Shake, substitute 1/4 cup peeled and sliced fresh kiwifruit for the raspberries and proceed as directed above. Garnish with peeled and sliced fresh kiwifruit.

Chocolate-Pistachio Shake

The great tastes of chocolate and pistachio mix well in this drink.

1 cup milk
2 scoops pistachio ice cream
1 teaspoon unsweetened cocoa powder

Whipped cream (optional)
Ground pistachio nuts, raw or roasted, unsalted, for garnish (optional)

Mix the milk, ice cream, and cocoa powder in a blender for 15 to 20 seconds, or until smooth. Pour into a tall glass and top with whipped cream and sprinkle with ground pistachio nuts, if desired.

Serves 1

White Chocolate-Vanilla Shake

This beautiful white drink is like a vanilla milkshake with the flavor of white chocolate in it. Drink it right away while it is still frothy.

2 tablespoons white chocolate chips	1½ cups milk
	2 scoops vanilla ice cream

Stir the chocolate chips into the milk in a saucepan over low heat for 5 to 6 minutes, or until hot (do not boil). Chill in the refrigerator and mix with the ice cream in a blender for 15 to 20 seconds, or until smooth.

Serves 2

Variation: For a White Chocolate–Chocolate Shake, substitute chocolate ice cream for the vanilla ice cream. Proceed as directed above.

Vanilla-Chocolate-Orange
Shake

The vanilla, chocolate, and orange flavors mix beautifully in this drink. Feel free to substitute 1 cup chocolate ice cream for the vanilla ice cream and cocoa powder.

1 cup vanilla ice cream
½ cup orange juice

1 teaspoon unsweetened
cocoa powder

Mix all the ingredients in a blender for 15 to 20 seconds, or until smooth.

Serves 1

Variations: For a Vanilla-Chocolate-Tangerine Shake, substitute ½ cup tangerine juice for the orange juice. Proceed as directed above.

For a Vanilla-Chocolate-Lemon Shake, substitute 1 tablespoon lemon juice for the orange juice. Proceed as directed above.

Chocolate-Pineapple-Coconut Shake

Pineapple and coconut add a tropical accent to this chocolate shake!

2 scoops chocolate ice cream	Whipped cream (optional)
¼ cup coconut milk	Sweetened shredded coconut or pineapple
¼ cup pineapple juice	slices, for garnish
½ cup milk	(optional)

Mix the ice cream, coconut milk, pineapple juice, and milk in a blender for 15 to 20 seconds, or until smooth. Pour into 2 tall glasses and top with whipped cream and garnish with sweetened shredded coconut or slices of pineapple, if desired.

Serves 2

Chocolate-Lemon Sherbet Shake

This low-cal shake is a great refresher for a hot summer afternoon!

1 cup lemon sherbet
½ cup milk, nonfat

1 teaspoon unsweetened cocoa powder

Mix all the ingredients in a blender for 15 to 20 seconds, or until smooth.

Serves 1

Variations: For a Chocolate–Lime Sherbet Shake, substitute 1 cup lime sherbet for the lemon sherbet and proceed as directed above.

For a Chocolate–Orange Sherbet Shake, substitute 1 cup orange sherbet for the lemon sherbet and proceed as directed above.

Chocolate Malted Shake

Please feel free to substitute 2 scoops of vanilla ice cream and 1 tablespoon unsweetened cocoa powder for the chocolate ice cream in this drink—which is a classic!

2 scoops chocolate ice cream

1 cup milk

1 tablespoon malted milk powder

Whipped cream (optional)

Sweetened chocolate powder (optional)

Mix the ice cream, milk, and malted milk powder in a blender for 15 to 20 seconds, or until smooth. Pour into a tall glass and top with whipped cream and chocolate powder, if desired.

Serves 1

Variations: For a Banana-Chocolate Malted Shake, add ½ peeled and sliced banana to the ice cream, milk, and malted milk powder. Proceed as directed above. Garnish with peeled and sliced banana, if desired.

For a Banana-Strawberry-Chocolate Malted Shake, add ¼ peeled and sliced banana and 4 strawberries to the ice cream, milk, and malted milk powder. Proceed as directed above. Garnish with peeled and sliced banana and/or a fresh strawberry, if desired.

Vanilla-Mint-Chocolate
Malted Shake

Enjoy this minty-malty refresher while you are sitting by the pool in the summer.

1 cup milk

2 scoops vanilla ice cream

⅛ teaspoon mint extract

1 tablespoon unsweetened cocoa powder

1 teaspoon malted milk powder

Whipped cream (optional)

Sweetened chocolate powder (optional)

Mix the milk, ice cream, mint extract, cocoa powder, and malted milk powder in a blender for 15 to 20 seconds, or until smooth. Pour into a tall glass and top with whipped cream and chocolate powder, if desired.

Serves 1

Chocolate Chip Cookie Shake

If you blend this drink for a shorter time, you will have larger pieces of chocolate chip cookie in it.

1 cup milk

2 scoops chocolate ice cream

4 chocolate chip cookies

Whipped cream (optional)

Additional chocolate chip cookie, for garnish (optional)

Mix the milk, ice cream, and 4 cookies in a blender for 10 to 15 seconds, or until smooth. Pour into a tall glass and top with whipped cream and garnish with a chocolate chip cookie, if desired.

Serves 1

Chocolate-Peanut Butter Shake

Chocolate and peanut butter is a classic combination—enjoy!

2 scoops chocolate ice
  cream
½ cup milk
1 tablespoon peanut
  butter, creamy

Unsalted, roasted
peanuts, for garnish
(optional)

Mix the ice cream, milk, and peanut butter in a blender for 15 to 20 seconds, or until smooth. Pour into a tall glass and garnish with peanuts, if desired.

Serves 1

Variation: For a Vanilla-Chocolate–Peanut Butter Shake, substitute 2 scoops of vanilla ice cream and 1 teaspoon unsweetened cocoa powder for the chocolate ice cream. Proceed as directed above.

Gourmet *Chocolate* Drinks *with* Liquor

Hot *Gourmet* Chocolate *Drinks* with *Liquor*

Crème de Cacao Hot Chocolate

Chocolate! Chocolate! Chocolate! From the top to the bottom!

$\frac{1}{2}$ ounce unsweetened
   baking chocolate
1 cup milk
2 tablespoons crème de
   cacao

$\frac{1}{4}$ cup heavy cream,
   whipped
Sweetened chocolate
   powder

Stir the chocolate into the milk in a saucepan over low heat for 3 to 4 minutes, or until hot (do not boil). Pour into a mug, add the crème de cacao, and top with whipped cream and chocolate powder.

Serves 1

Rum Hot Chocolate

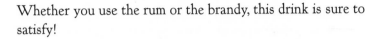

Whether you use the rum or the brandy, this drink is sure to satisfy!

$^1\!/_2$ ounce semisweet baking chocolate

1 cup milk

2 tablespoons rum

$^1\!/_4$ cup heavy cream, whipped

Ground nutmeg

Stir the chocolate into the milk in a saucepan over low heat for 3 to 4 minutes, or until hot (do not boil). Pour into a mug, add the rum, and top with whipped cream and nutmeg.

Serves 1

Variation: For a Brandy Hot Chocolate, substitute 2 tablespoons brandy for the rum and proceed as directed above.

Grand Marnier Hot Chocolate

The Grand Marnier bursts into your mouth along with the chocolate in this very tasty drink, and the orange peel on top adds just the right touch.

1 tablespoon chocolate
syrup
1 cup milk
2 tablespoons Grand
Marnier liqueur

$\frac{1}{4}$ cup heavy cream,
whipped
Grated orange peel, for
garnish

Stir the chocolate syrup into the milk in a saucepan over low heat for 3 to 4 minutes, or until hot (do not boil). Pour into a mug, add the Grand Marnier, top with whipped cream, and sprinkle with grated orange peel.

Serves 1

Variation: For an Amaretto Hot Chocolate, substitute 2 tablespoons of amaretto liqueur for the Grand Marnier and substitute ground almonds for the grated orange peel. Proceed as directed above.

Anisette Hot Chocolate

This one is a great after-dinner drink—like a dessert in itself!

$\frac{1}{2}$ ounce semisweet baking
  chocolate
1 cup milk
2 tablespoons anisette
  liqueur

$\frac{1}{4}$ cup heavy cream,
  whipped
1 piece red or black
  licorice, for garnish
  (optional)

Stir the chocolate into the milk in a saucepan over low heat
for 3 to 4 minutes, or until hot (do not boil). Pour into a mug,
add the anisette, top with whipped cream, and garnish with
a piece of licorice, if desired.

Serves 1

237

Whiskey Hot Cocoa

Warm your spirits–along with your insides–with this whiskey-flavored hot cocoa drink!

1 teaspoon unsweetened
  cocoa powder
1 teaspoon sugar
1 cup milk
⅛ teaspoon ground
  cinnamon

1 tablespoon whiskey
¼ cup heavy cream,
  whipped
Additional ground
  cinnamon

Stir the cocoa powder and sugar into 2 teaspoons of the milk in a saucepan, until a smooth paste is formed. Add the rest of the milk and ⅛ teaspoon cinnamon and stir the mixture constantly over low heat for 3 to 4 minutes, or until it is hot (do not boil). Pour into a mug, add the whiskey, and top with whipped cream and cinnamon.

Serves 1

Chartreuse Hot Chocolate

The Chartreuse and the pistachio nuts complement each other nicely in this drink.

½ ounce semisweet baking chocolate	¼ cup heavy cream, whipped
1 cup milk	Ground pistachio nuts,
1 tablespoon green Chartreuse liqueur	raw or roasted, unsalted, for garnish

Stir the chocolate into the milk in a saucepan over low heat for 3 to 4 minutes, or until hot (do not boil). Pour into a mug, add the Chartreuse, and top with the whipped cream and pistachio nuts.

Serves 1

Chambord Hot Chocolate

The taste of the raspberry liqueur is enhanced by the fresh raspberries in this drink.

$\frac{1}{2}$ ounce semisweet baking
  chocolate
1 cup milk
1 tablespoon Chambord
  liqueur

$\frac{1}{4}$ cup heavy cream,
  whipped
Fresh raspberries, for
  garnish

Stir the chocolate into the milk in a saucepan over low heat for 3 to 4 minutes, or until hot (do not boil). Pour into a mug, add the Chambord, top with whipped cream, and garnish with fresh raspberries.

Serves 1

Variation: For a Chambord–White Hot Chocolate, substitute 1 tablespoon white chocolate chips for the semisweet chocolate and proceed as directed above.

Amaretto-Kahlúa
Hot Chocolate

This almond-coffee hot chocolate provides a great combination of tastes.

$^1/_2$ *ounce semisweet baking*
chocolate
1 *cup milk*
1 *tablespoon amaretto*
liqueur
1 *tablespoon Kahlúa*
liqueur

$^1/_4$ *cup heavy cream,*
whipped
Ground cinnamon or
sweetened chocolate
powder

Stir the chocolate into the milk in a saucepan over low heat for 3 to 4 minutes, or until hot (do not boil). Pour into a mug, add the amaretto and Kahlúa, top with whipped cream, and sprinkle with cinnamon or chocolate powder.

Serves 1

Variation: For a Brandy-Kahlúa Hot Chocolate, substitute 1 tablespoon brandy for the amaretto and proceed as directed above.

Brandy-Grand Marnier
Hot Chocolate

The brandy adds a nice accent to the orange flavor of the Grand Marnier in this drink.

½ ounce semisweet baking
chocolate
1 cup milk
1 tablespoon brandy
1 tablespoon Grand
Marnier liqueur

¼ cup heavy cream,
whipped
Grated orange peel, for
garnish

Stir the chocolate into the milk in a saucepan for 3 to 4 minutes, or until hot (do not boil). Pour into a mug, add the brandy and Grand Marnier, and top with whipped cream and grated orange peel.

Serves 1

Bailey's-Frangelico Hot Chocolate

The distinctive taste of the Bailey's mixes well with the Frangelico in this drink—and it tastes great with the amaretto too!

$^1/_2$ ounce unsweetened
baking chocolate
1 cup milk
2 tablespoons Bailey's
Original Irish Cream
liqueur

1 tablespoon Frangelico
liqueur
$^1/_4$ cup heavy cream,
whipped
Sweetened chocolate
powder

Stir the chocolate into the milk in a saucepan over low heat for 3 to 4 minutes, or until hot (do not boil). Pour into a mug, add the Bailey's and Frangelico, and top with whipped cream and chocolate powder.

Serves 1

Variation: For a Bailey's-Amaretto Hot Chocolate, substitute 1 tablespoon amaretto liqueur for the Frangelico and proceed as directed above.

Whiskey-Coconut Hot Chocolate

Bring the taste of the tropics to your palate with this marvelous drink!

$\frac{1}{2}$ ounce unsweetened
  baking chocolate
2 tablespoons coconut
  milk
1 teaspoon sugar
1 cup milk

1 tablespoon whiskey
$\frac{1}{4}$ cup heavy cream,
  whipped
Sweetened shredded
  coconut, for garnish

Stir the chocolate, coconut milk, and sugar into the milk in a saucepan over low heat for 3 to 4 minutes, or until hot (do not boil). Pour into a mug, add the whiskey, and top with whipped cream and sweetened shredded coconut.

Serves 1

Grand Marnier-Frangelico Hot Cocoa

The orange, hazelnut, and chocolate flavors, when sipped through whipped cream, are a real delight!

1 teaspoon unsweetened
   cocoa powder
1 cup milk
1 tablespoon Grand
   Marnier liqueur
1 tablespoon Frangelico
   liqueur

¼ cup heavy cream,
   whipped
Grated orange peel or
   ground hazelnuts, for
   garnish

Stir the cocoa powder into 2 teaspoons of the milk in a saucepan, until a smooth paste is formed. Add the rest of the milk and stir the mixture constantly over low heat for 3 to 4 minutes, or until it is hot (do not boil). Pour into a mug, add the Grand Marnier and Frangelico, and top with whipped cream and orange peel or hazelnuts.

Serves 1

Variation: For a Grand Marnier–Crème de Menthe Hot Cocoa, substitute 1 tablespoon crème de menthe for the Frangelico and proceed as directed above. Garnish with grated orange peel or a fresh mint sprig.

Crème de Menthe-Kahlúa Hot Cocoa

The mint provides a nice accent for the Kahlúa in this drink.

1 teaspoon unsweetened
cocoa powder
1 cup milk
1 tablespoon crème de
menthe

1 tablespoon Kahlúa
liqueur
¼ cup heavy cream,
whipped
Fresh mint sprig, for
garnish

Stir the cocoa powder into 2 teaspoons of the milk in a saucepan, until a smooth paste is formed. Pour the rest of the milk into the saucepan and stir the mixture constantly over low heat for 3 to 4 minutes, or until it is hot (do not boil). Pour into a mug, add the crème de menthe and Kahlúa, top with whipped cream, and garnish with a fresh mint sprig.

Serves 1

Frangelico-White
Hot Chocolate

What a combination of tastes—white chocolate, Frangelico, whipped cream, and hazelnuts—all in a pretty white package!

1 tablespoon white
 chocolate chips
1 cup milk
2 tablespoons Frangelico
 liqueur

¼ cup heavy cream,
 whipped
Ground hazelnuts, for
 garnish

Stir the chocolate chips into the milk in a saucepan over low heat for 3 to 4 minutes, or until hot (do not boil). Pour into a mug, add the Frangelico, and top with whipped cream and ground hazelnuts.

Serves 1

Whiskey-Rum-White
Hot Chocolate

This white drink will warm you up on a cold winter night, in front of a fire.

1 tablespoon white
   chocolate chips
1 cup milk
1 tablespoon whiskey

1 tablespoon rum
1/4 cup heavy cream,
   whipped

Stir the chocolate chips into the milk in a saucepan over low heat for 3 to 4 minutes, or until hot (do not boil). Pour into a mug, add the whiskey and rum, and top with whipped cream.

Serves 1

Crème de Cacao-Brandy-
Kahlúa Hot Cocoa

The crème de cacao, brandy, and Kahlúa mix together in this drink to create a very special taste.

1 teaspoon unsweetened
  cocoa powder
1 cup milk
1 teaspoon crème de cacao
1 teaspoon brandy

1 tablespoon Kahlúa
  liqueur
¼ cup heavy cream,
  whipped
  Sweetened chocolate
  powder

Stir the cocoa powder into 2 teaspoons of the milk in a saucepan, until a smooth paste is formed. Pour the rest of the milk into the saucepan and stir the mixture constantly over low heat for 3 to 4 minutes, or until it is hot (do not boil). Pour into a mug, add the crème de cacao, brandy, and Kahlúa, and top with whipped cream and chocolate powder.

Serves 1

Brandy-Rum-Coffee
Hot Chocolate

The coffee-chocolate mixture combined with the brandy and rum makes a great assortment of tastes.

$1/2$ ounce semisweet baking
  chocolate
$1/2$ cup milk
$1/2$ cup freshly brewed
  coffee, still piping hot
1 tablespoon brandy

1 tablespoon rum
$1/4$ cup heavy cream,
  whipped
Sweetened chocolate
  powder

Stir the chocolate into the milk and coffee in a saucepan over low heat for 3 to 4 minutes, or until hot (do not boil). Pour into a mug, add the brandy and rum, and top with whipped cream and chocolate powder.

Serves 1

Crème de Cacao-Amaretto Hot Cocoa Eggnog

The crème de cacao and amaretto add a unique accent to this eggnog mixture.

1 teaspoon unsweetened
  cocoa powder
$\frac{1}{2}$ cup eggnog
$\frac{1}{2}$ cup milk
1 teaspoon crème de cacao

1 teaspoon amaretto
  liqueur
$\frac{1}{4}$ cup heavy cream,
  whipped
Ground nutmeg

Stir the cocoa powder into 2 teaspoons of the eggnog in a saucepan, until a smooth paste is formed. Pour the rest of the eggnog along with the milk into the saucepan and stir the mixture constantly over low heat for 3 to 4 minutes, or until hot (do not boil). Pour into a mug, add the crème de cacao and amaretto, and top with whipped cream and nutmeg.

Serves 1

Variation: For a Rum Hot Cocoa Eggnog, substitute 1 teaspoon rum for the crème de cacao and the amaretto. Proceed as directed above.

Cold *Gourmet* Chocolate *Drinks* with *Liquor*

Crème de Cacao-Frangelico Delight

This white drink features the taste of chocolate from the crème de cacao, along with a hazelnut accent from the Frangelico–scrumptious!

2 tablespoons crème de cacao

1 tablespoon Frangelico liqueur

1 cup milk
Ice cubes

¼ cup heavy cream, whipped

Sweetened chocolate powder or ground hazelnuts, for garnish

Stir the crème de cacao and Frangelico into the milk and pour over ice in a tall glass. Top with whipped cream and chocolate powder or hazelnuts.

Serves 1

Variations: For a Crème de Cacao–Rum Delight, substitute 1 tablespoon rum for the Frangelico and proceed as directed above. Garnish with sweetened chocolate powder.

For a Crème de Cacao–Grand Marnier Delight, substitute 1 tablespoon Grand Marnier liqueur for the Frangelico and proceed as directed above. Garnish with sweetened chocolate powder or grated orange peel.

Tea-Frangelico Chocolate Delight

The Frangelico provides a hazelnut aftertaste in this drink—a
great refresher!

⅓ cup brewed English
   Breakfast or another
   black tea, chilled
1 tablespoon chocolate
   syrup
1 teaspoon Frangelico
   liqueur

⅔ cup milk
  Ice cubes
  Whipped cream
  (optional)
  Sweetened chocolate
  powder (optional)

Stir the tea, chocolate syrup, and Frangelico into the milk
and pour over ice in a tall glass. Top with whipped cream
and chocolate powder, if desired.

Serves 1

Chocolate-Mint Ice Cream Float

The chocolate and mint liqueurs make a refreshing contribution to this drink—and the chocolate ice cream gives you an extra "punch" as well.

1 tablespoon crème de cacao

1 tablespoon crème de menthe

¾ cup milk
Ice cubes

1 scoop chocolate ice cream

¼ cup heavy cream, whipped

Sweetened chocolate powder

Fresh mint sprig, for garnish

Stir the crème de cacao and the crème de menthe into the milk and pour over ice in a tall glass. Add the ice cream, top with whipped cream, sprinkle with chocolate powder, and garnish with a fresh mint sprig.

Serves 1

Crème de Cacao Soda

The crème de cacao gives your cola an extra "zing," along with the great taste of chocolate.

- ³⁄₄ cup cola
- ¹⁄₄ cup carbonated water
  - Ice cubes
- 2 tablespoons crème de cacao

- ¹⁄₄ cup heavy cream, whipped
  - Sweetened chocolate powder

Pour the cola and carbonated water over ice in a tall glass. Add the crème de cacao and top with whipped cream and chocolate powder.

Serves 1

Crème de Cacao-Raspberry Yogurt Blend

The crème de cacao sweetens this drink and gives it its chocolate taste.

½ cup plain yogurt, low-fat
½ cup milk, nonfat
½ cup fresh raspberries

2 tablespoons crème de cacao

Mix all the ingredients in a blender for 15 to 20 seconds, or until smooth.

Serves 1

Variations: For a Crème de Cacao–Blueberry Yogurt Blend, substitute ½ cup fresh blueberries for the raspberries and proceed as directed above.

For a Crème de Cacao–Strawberry Yogurt Blend, substitute ½ cup fresh strawberries for the raspberries and proceed as directed above.

Chocolate-Kirsch Yogurt Blend

The subtle taste of the kirsch (and the framboise) comes through in this low-cal pick-me-up.

$\frac{1}{2}$ cup cherry yogurt,
   low-fat
$\frac{1}{2}$ cup milk, nonfat

1 teaspoon unsweetened
   cocoa powder
1 tablespoon kirsch
   liqueur

Mix all the ingredients in a blender for 10 to 15 seconds, or until smooth.

Serves 1

Variation: For a Chocolate–Framboise Yogurt Blend, substitute $\frac{1}{2}$ cup raspberry yogurt for the cherry yogurt and substitute 1 tablespoon framboise liqueur for the kirsch liqueur. Proceed as directed above.

Crème de Cacao-Banana Crush

Enjoy this slushy, banana-tasting treat on a hot day!

1 scoop chocolate ice
cream
½ cup milk
1 tablespoon crème de
cacao
1 tablespoon banana
liqueur

¼ cup crushed ice
Whipped cream
(optional)
Banana, peeled and
sliced, for garnish
(optional)

Mix the ice cream, milk, crème de cacao, banana liqueur, and crushed ice in a blender for 15 to 20 seconds, or until smooth. Pour into a tall glass and top with whipped cream and banana slices, if desired.

Serves 1

Rum-Chocolate Shake

Whether you drink this one all by itself or sip it through whipped cream, it is sure to satisfy!

¹⁄₂ cup milk	Whipped cream
1 scoop chocolate ice	(optional)
cream	Sweetened chocolate
2 tablespoons rum	powder (optional)

Mix all the ingredients in a blender for 10 to 15 seconds, or until smooth. Pour into a tall glass and top with whipped cream and chocolate powder, if desired.

Serves 1

Chocolate-Crème de Menthe Shake

The crème de menthe adds a delightful, minty accent to this chocolate shake.

1 scoop chocolate ice
  cream
½ cup milk
1 tablespoon crème de
  menthe

Ice cubes
¼ cup heavy cream,
  whipped
Fresh mint sprig, for
  garnish

Mix the ice cream, milk, and crème de menthe in a blender for 15 to 20 seconds, or until smooth. Pour over ice, top with whipped cream, and garnish with a fresh mint sprig.

Serves 1

Strawberry-Amaretto
Chocolate Shake

The strawberry-almond taste of this drink combines well
with the chocolate taste of the cocoa powder–delightful!

½ cup milk

1 scoop vanilla ice cream

¼ cup fresh strawberries

1 teaspoon unsweetened
  cocoa powder

1 tablespoon amaretto
  liqueur

Whipped cream
(optional)

Additional fresh straw-
berries or sliced
almonds, for garnish
(optional)

Mix the milk, ice cream, ¼ cup strawberries, cocoa powder,
and amaretto in a blender for 15 to 20 seconds, or until
smooth. Pour into a tall glass and top with whipped cream
and garnish with fresh strawberries or sliced almonds, if
desired.

Serves 1

Index